To our son, Brad.
You are more than I ever prayed for,
and I thank God from my heart for you, my son.
How very proud I am of you—
a great man,
a caring husband,
a terrific father to our grandsons,
and a man after God's own heart.
I love you deeply and dearly.

Hugs,
Mom

I love you, I hope this will be a help to you. The Word of God is our only comfort, but sometimes it's nice to know what others have learned.

Contents

My Prayers for Rainy Seasons

$\mathcal{S}$till raining!

I stood at the window of our snug little motel room and watched the wind-blown water hammer the parking lot, just as it had hammered us from the time we left southern California a week before.

This, apparently, was the El Niño weather pattern we had been warned about all year. For some reason that nobody seemed to fully understand, warm water in the Pacific had shifted the ocean currents in a way that brought torrential rains and flooding to our state. Northern California, where my husband, Bob, and I had gone for a bit of relaxation between seminars, was especially hard hit, as we had discovered firsthand.

For days now, we had driven ahead of major floods, our car radio advising us of road closings and high water in towns we had just left. Hurricane-force winds had buffeted our van and whipped the normally tranquil bays we passed into whitecapped seas. Sheets of wind-blown rain had cut visibility on bridges and highways to almost nothing and kept my Bob's knuckles white on the steering wheel.

Finally we had taken refuge in this quaint little motel on Bodega Bay. Grateful for our charming room and the fireplace, we had built a fire, settled in, and waited for the deluge to stop.

But it never did, at least not while we were there.

Every day, all day and into the night, it rained.

And rained.

And rained.

For us southern Californians, accustomed to sunny skies and scanty rainfall, that experience was a sobering and miserable reminder of the reality behind the old saying, "When it rains it pours."

In this soggy El Niño year, when it rained it poured . . . and flooded . . . and blew, leaving us exhausted and drained and yearning for a bit of sunshine.

And though the rain was a novelty for us, those feelings were familiar.

For the last four or five years, you see, we've been living a "when it rains it pours" kind of life.

For me they have been the dark years, the overcast years, the years when one thing after another seemed to go wrong, when just as I knew things were getting better, something else hit.

Have you ever had times like that in your life?

Most likely you have—but if you haven't, you will.

That's not a threat, just a gentle reminder that in this world, to paraphrase a painfully blunt bumper sticker, things happen.

Bad things happen to good people. Thieves break through and steal. Earthquakes and floods and hurricanes strike. Arms and legs and hearts break. Viruses invade, healthy cells turn malignant. Banks fail. People die.

It's all part of the package of being human. All of us, if we live life long enough, will go through some kind of suffering, and some of us will suffer a lot.

Surely that's why "When it rains it pours" became a well-known saying in the first place—because it's so often true! Sooner or later, in everybody's life, some rain must fall, and it seems that one thunderstorm always leads to another . . . and another. One storm cloud moves in before you have a chance to dry out from the previous one, and then the rain seems to settle in and stay until you can't even remember a day without drizzle.

As I said, rain has been in our family forecast for quite awhile now. Many have been the times when I truly felt I could not go on—although, with God's help, I did, and that is part of the story, too. In fact, it is the very heart of the story: the gracious and wonderful ways that God has worked to change my heart and my circumstances for the better in the midst of my pain and struggle.

A few years back, at the beginning of this difficult time, when I had little inkling just how difficult things would get (or how those difficulties would help me grow), I wrote a devotional book called *Fill My Cup, Lord*. It was based on the idea that we must depend on our heavenly Father to fill the "cups" of our lives with what we need to please him and live full lives—quietness, encouragement, forgiveness, trust, communion, strength, thanksgiving, and service. It also stressed that we must learn to empty our cups of negatives such as stress, criticism, and selfishness before we can be filled with God's good things.

But what do you do when the negatives in your life seem to fill your cup faster than you can empty them out? What do you do when your cup seems to overflow with trouble?

Even when you know the right things to do—pray, confess, give it to God, trust him, praise him, thank him—how do you keep on when the rain just doesn't seem to stop? How do you keep your head above water when the floods surround you?

Those questions have literally been the theme of my life the past few years. And the answers I have lived myself into have both comforted and astonished me.

I have been surprised by what held steady under the deluge and what was swept away. I have been amazed at the changes that have occurred in me and my family as a result. Not only have my eyes been opened to the reality of suffering all around me, but also to the heart-lifting reality that God is constantly working, amidst all the pain in this world, to turn brokeness into beauty.

Most of all, I have been warmed and upheld by a deepening knowledge of just how steady a rock my heavenly Father is, how my relationship with him has grown deeper and stronger and more meaningful than I ever thought possible.

I want that for you too.

Whether the rain in your own life is a steady, wearying drizzle, a dramatic deluge, or just a threatening cloud on the horizon, I want you to know that God's purpose in it all is to draw you closer into his warm embrace and then use you to draw others to him as well.

It is my prayer that these words will give you strength and courage and encouragement for facing your own rainy seasons, both present and future, that they will increase your thirst for the blessings that God can provide, even in times of one problem after another.

Especially in times of one problem after another.

For even though my cup has overflowed with trouble in recent years, I can still honestly say that, through it all, my cup has continually overflowed with the goodness and mercy of my God.

In this book I want to tell you why.

It's Too Much, Lord!

It's too much, Lord!
Just one thing after another—
too much pain, too much worry,
too much sadness,
too many hard days and endless nights,
and I'm just so tired . . .
Lord, It's just too much.
Help!

1

It's Too Much, Lord!

A Cup Overflowing with Trouble—and Love

"And after you have suffered . . ."
—I Peter 5:10

I never thought it would happen to me.

But then, most of us never do.

Yes, we know there will be times of pain and difficulty and sadness. The Bible is quite blunt about it: "In this world," said Jesus, "you will have trouble." Years later, the apostle Peter wrote that we shouldn't be surprised by suffering or think it an abnormal thing.

But still, we *are* surprised when bad things happen to us.

At some level, I guess, we all believe we will be an exception, that the pain and suffering that infect the world will somehow bypass us. Or if we've already endured times of pain, we assume we've somehow been inoculated to avoid further trauma.

But life simply doesn't work that way.

Have you found that out, too?

In this world, difficulty is part of the general forecast. Sometimes the trouble comes in torrents. And although we have been told to expect it, as often as not it seems to hit from an unexpected angle.

That's how it felt to me. I should have known better. But I never saw it coming.

Just so you'll know the background, I want to tell you the outlines of my story. But even as I tell it, I'm aware that your story may top mine. You may have known far more pain and fear and worry in your circumstances, or you may know someone whose pain and fear and worry make mine look almost petty. *I* know people like this—people whose stories leave me humbled and amazed.

But I'm not writing to swap war stories. I am writing to testify to what I have learned from a God who promises to bring us through floods undrowned, through fires unburned. Besides, I have learned over the years that each person's trouble is unique to him or her, but that in sharing our stories we can often find common ground. So let me tell you just a little about the years when my cup overflowed with trouble, hoping that, somehow, the telling will help you in your own pain and encourage you to tell your own story.

For me, the "dark years" all started four years ago when our daughter, our precious Jenny, took her three young children and left her husband.

I was devastated. I never thought something like that could happen in our family.

Yes, I knew all about the divorce rate in our society. I was well aware that even Christian homes are not immune. But now my own family, so precious to my heart, so lovingly nurtured over the years, was being ripped apart. And when that happened, something deep inside of me ruptured as well.

On the one hand, I knew that my daughter had been deeply unhappy. And yet I believed so strongly in the sanctity of marriage. I was convinced that, with work and attention, even a difficult marriage could survive. (I still believe these things, with all my heart.) I hurt for my son-in-law, who seemed devastated by my daughter's departure. My heart bled for those three children, my grandchildren, who loved their mother and daddy and wanted only for their home to be whole again. And I was full of fear and worry for my Jenny, who seemed so angry and rebellious and far from being the kind of mother those children needed.

You see, when our Jenny left her husband, she left her God as well.

And I, who spoke about happy homes to hundreds of women a week, was helpless to do anything about the breakup of this home and the pain of these people I loved so very deeply.

Even now, it's hard for me to express the depth of the anguish I felt over this circumstance. I wanted with every fiber of my body for that broken home to be healed, for the pain to be erased from my grandchildren's faces, for my daughter and son-in-law to find each other again.

And it just wasn't happening.

Weeks passed, then months, then years, and the reality of that broken home didn't change—although, as I would see later, God was working to redeem the situation in surprising ways. Meanwhile, either coincidentally or because of the stress, I began to get sick.

It began with chronic bouts of bronchitis, one of those irritating illnesses where you cough and cough and don't seem to get better. Series after series of antibiotics didn't seem to help. Neither did sinus surgery. Referred to an allergist, I was soon taking three allergy shots a week.

And that was only the beginning. The bronchitis persisted, along with other strange symptoms, such as mosquito bites that itched fiercely and refused to heal. I had gained a little weight, and though I "cleaned up" pretty well for seminars, I was beginning to think that something was seriously wrong with me.

Through this all, though, I continued with my busy schedule of giving *More Hours in My Day* seminars. I wrote books. I even began, tentatively, to share my pain about Jenny in both the seminars and the books. Women were responding. My ministry was growing.

And all the while, I was doing everything I knew to get better. You see, I'm the kind of person who has always been teased for my healthy lifestyle. I take vitamins. I eat right and exercise regularly. I've even coauthored a book on healthy eating! Now, faced with illness, I redoubled my efforts. I watched my diet carefully and took a lot of vitamins, applying everything I knew about good nutrition. I showed up faithfully for my allergy shots. I took full advantage of our summer and winter rest periods and tried to get enough sleep. I carefully researched the many books and tapes sent to me by concerned friends, and I followed the suggestions of the ones that seemed sound.

Finally, when nothing seemed to help, I dug out a name that I had jotted down at a conference years before. A sweet woman in Arkansas had shared the name of a nutritional consultant in our area, a Christian woman with a Ph.D. in nutrition and a specialization in homeopathic remedies. I called this "health doctor" and made an appointment. And on my very first visit I sensed that this woman was part of God's plan for my healing.

We talked at length about what had been happening to me, what I had been doing to help myself, and what treatments my doctors had described. And I shared with this health doctor something that I had begun to notice—that I actually felt better in the weeks when I missed my allergy shots. Working together, she and I finally determined that the combination of antibiotics and allergy shots and perhaps other factors I didn't know of had combined to poison my system. I was experiencing toxic overload. My immune system was at zero, and my body had reached the point where it could not even assimilate the vitamins and minerals I was putting into it.

Now, I want to make something very clear at this point. I am *not* saying that traditional allergy treatments are harmful or that homeopathic treatment is better than traditional medicine. I am not even saying that my medical doctors were wrong and my health doctor was right. Every body is different, and I believe God heals each of us in different ways: through traditional medicine, through alternative medicine, even through spontaneous healing. As I visited this nutritional consultant, however, I felt a strong confirmation in my spirit that the path she pointed to was the right path for me to take. So I made the decision to quit my allergy-shot regimen, and with the nutritionist's help I began a program of detoxifying my body through diet.

I thought it was working, though the process itself was not pleasant. The very process of ridding one's body of toxins can involve quite a bit of discomfort: nausea, excessive perspiration, and other unpleasant sensations. But I thought I could feel my healthy, carefully chosen diet working. I began losing some weight—again, I was sure, because of the diet. And in some ways I could feel myself growing stronger. For a few months I was even free of the bronchitis. But then it returned with a vengeance, along with chills, vomiting, and fever.

Somehow, through it all, God was still giving me the strength I needed to do what he had called me to do: to get up on that platform and speak, and to talk and minister to women afterward. So many times I would stand by that platform wondering if I would even be able to climb the steps. And then God would take over and do his work, and I would speak and my heart would swell to see the work God was doing in the lives of the women at that seminar. Even in my depleted state, I rejoiced in what God was doing. But I also knew something was deeply wrong with my body, and I still didn't know what it was.

My weight loss continued and accelerated. People began to comment on how thin I looked. I suffered with night sweats and nausea, and I still couldn't stop coughing.

Then finally my family put their foot down.

My daughter Jenny made me an appointment to see a doctor, who took some tests and then referred me to a Christian oncologist. And after a round of blood tests and other diagnostics we had a name for the illness that was behind so many of my symptoms: chronic lymphatic leukemia.

Cancer.

The very name was terrifying. And now the doctors were talking about further tests and treatments involving radiation and chemotherapy. They explained that though this particular form of leukemia moves relatively slowly and that I could live with it a long time, it was still very serious and needed to be treated right away. I needed some tests involving radiation, and then I needed to start a program of chemotherapy.

After my previous experience, my very soul shrank from the thought of these procedures, which involved injecting more chemicals into my body. So I went to my health doctor for advice. I sat there in her office, weeping and shaking and painfully thin, and I told her what the diagnosis had been.

What she said was, "Give me two weeks." She asked me to wait at least that long before I agreed to any more tests or treatment. "If you let them subject your body to all that," she said, "you risk undoing everything we've worked so hard to do. So at least give me two weeks to prepare you and build you up for treatment."

Now I was heartsick, pulled between the advice of my health doctor, whom I respected so deeply; my oncologist, whom I had also grown to trust; my family, who loved me and wanted me to be well; and my own desire not to fill my body full of chemicals again. So I prayed, and I talked to friends, and I prayed some more, and I finally told my Bob I wanted to give my health doctor the two weeks she requested. I expected him to resist, but to my surprise he agreed.

It turned out to be more than two weeks. The combination of holidays and commitments kept me away from that doctor's office until six weeks later. Meanwhile, I had begun a special diet and a course of homeopathic treatment to build up my body. I had been asking for prayer from everyone I knew. My health doctor and my oncologist were praying for me. My friends were praying for me. Women I met at conferences were praying for me, and I received cards and letters from people I didn't even know who had learned what I was going through and promised me their prayers. I knew I was being surrounded by a powerful prayer shield.

And then I went back to my Christian oncologist, bracing myself for the tests and treatments I feared.

Before he started, though, he tested my blood again. And with a look of surprise on his face he asked me, "What have you been doing? This is very impressive."

Then he told me that my white blood cell count, which had been very high six weeks earlier, was now almost normal, and well out of the danger range. My other indicators had subsided as well.

"It was prayer," I told him with wonder. "Prayer and homeopathic treatments."

That good Christian man just looked at me. "I believe in prayer," he said, "and I have no problem with alternative treatments. I suggest you just keep doing what you're doing." He also said, "I see no reason to proceed with the tests and the chemotherapy at this time."

Hallelujah! What a victory. We left that office praising God almost hysterically. Vastly relieved, I rejoiced that God was healing me, and I dedicated myself to rest and build up my strength for yet another busy fall season. Step by step, day by day, I could feel myself growing stronger, praising God, eager to get back to work . . . until that day a little more than two months later when I went to change the sheets on our bed and ended up doubled over in agony.

I had never felt such a pain as this searing and stabbing deep in my abdomen. I could barely make it to the couch to lie down. By the time Bob and Jenny loaded me into our van and headed for the hospital, I was curled into a fetal position, holding my stomach and moaning.

That night, I underwent emergency surgery for a perforated ulcer the size of a silver dollar.

I was in the hospital for more than a week. We had to cancel seven seminars, something I had not done during my whole long siege with bronchitis, chemical poisoning, or even leukemia. Bob was stressed with handling the details of our business and trying to take care of me. I had a book deadline staring me in the face. And Jenny's family was still not together!

My health doctor assured me (when I could speak again) that this was not a setback. But it felt like one, and just when I was finally getting better. Would life ever feel good again?

That was four months ago. And that, so far, is the story of my "rainy years," when my cup has overflowed with pain and fear and uncertainty and worry and weakness . . . but also with the miracles of God working in and through my life.

And the story still goes on. My stitches have healed, my bland ulcer diet has given way to my nutritionist's strength diet, I have resumed my conference schedule. Jenny and her husband have not reconciled, but God has worked other amazing miracles in my daughter's life in the meantime.

So things are better.

But just the other weekend I was terrified to feel another pain in my stomach, almost a reprise of that awful, searing ulcer pain.

It was not serious this time, just an excess of stomach acid.

But it was a sobering experience—a reminder that, ultimately, I am not in control of any of the things life pours into my cup. My troubles might well continue. I may never get well. My family may never be put back together the way it was before.

It could be one thing after another for the rest of my life. There is nothing I can do to keep my cup from overflowing with trouble.

Except for one thing.

There is one thing that I, and you, and anyone who is facing trouble can do and must do, again and again.

We can carry that overflowing cup, messy and sloppy as it is, to the foot of the cross and leave it there.

Through prayer, through holy imagination, through an act of the will, we can surrender that cup of pain to the Lord, so that he can deal with the overflow of trouble.

You see, the only antidote that I know for a cup overflowing with trouble is a cup overflowing with the love of Christ.

And he gives us that.

I knew it before I went through these years of agony, but now I know it in a far deeper part of my soul. I have felt his touch, his provision, at a cell level, deep in my being. I have witnessed his healing, redemptive power at work in my life even when things seemed darkest.

I have seen his work in the lives of others, as well, and that brings me hope and encouragement.

Not long ago, for example, I received a wonderful letter from a woman named Barbara who had grown up in a sexually abusive home. She cannot remember a time in her childhood when she was not abused. Barbara married and had a child but was widowed suddenly at age twenty-five. When she remarried, her first husband's parents disowned both her and her child.

Talk about years of trouble! But somehow, through all that, this woman was able to remain open to God's healing, or, as she puts it, "Jesus loved me through it all." She remarried and raised a family. Now, at age fifty-four, she is finishing graduate school with a degree in counseling and preparing to embark on a new career and a new ministry. She writes, "At this point in my life, God has a real call on my life. I haven't a clue where he is taking me, but I am enjoying the trip."

Or I think of a dear man we know, our former pastor, who has gone through one tragedy after another: the loss of his home to fire (twice!), the loss of a wife, who became an alcoholic and eventually committed suicide, and the loss of a son, who was paralyzed in an auto accident and died at an early age. Whenever I think of this man, who has endured so much, I am amazed by his gentle, compassionate spirit, his commitment to ministry, the underlying joy in his heart that could come only from having his cup filled by the Holy Spirit.

Again and again I have seen this happen—God working in the lives of men and women who bring their overflowing cups of suffering to him and allow him to refill their cups with his love. And again and again, even in the midst of my own suffering, I have seen him do it for me as well.

It hasn't always come the way I expected. One thing I have learned from this rainy season in my life is that God gives us what we need, not always what we want. He gives us what we need to grow and draw closer to him and accomplish his purposes, and my own peace and joy depend in part on accepting what he chooses to give me.

But that doesn't mean I have to *like* what life hands out to me!

I can't find any recommendation in God's Word that I'm supposed to be glad that my daughter's marriage is unhappy, that my grandchildren are torn in half, or that my body is sick and the doctors can't figure out what is wrong. I don't have to like the pain that sears my abdomen or the cancer that saps my strength.

I can pray to avoid suffering and even pray for it to be taken away. Jesus himself asked to be spared the cup of his own suffering and death.

And I'm not even required to refrain from complaining when my cup is full of suffering. Like Job or David, I can cry out to God and tell him exactly how I feel; I can even tell him I don't feel he's doing things right. The Psalms are absolutely filled with people fussing and fuming at God because life is not happening to them the way they would like it to happen. (One day, when I was feeling especially unhappy, I opened the book of Psalms and read page after page of "complaining" Psalms out loud to God!)

And somewhere along the line, of course, I inevitably found myself asking the *why* questions: Why me? Why now? Why me and not someone else?

I've asked those questions plenty of times, sometimes angrily, sometimes plaintively, sometimes with a sense of embarrassment.

Why embarrassment?

Because I really know the answer, of course.

Or at least I know the real question:

Why *not* me?

In this world, Jesus assures us, we *will* have trouble. He of all people knew what it was to suffer undeservedly. In all the pain I have suffered over the years, I have had but a tiny taste of what he went through on my account.

And yet, in the very next breath, Jesus reminds me that no matter what our pain, we still have a reason to hope.

"In this world you will have trouble," he said. "But take heart! I have overcome the world."

We shouldn't be surprised, Peter reminds us, when we have pain in our lives. That's the inevitable result of living here on this fallen planet in vulnerable bodies, with weak spirits and fallible souls. But Peter, near the end of his epistle, adds a ringing promise that picks up shine and polish and meaning for me each time I read it again. It's one of the verses that kept me hoping and moving forward when I felt like I couldn't go on.

"After you have suffered for a little while," the apostle writes, "the God of all grace, who has called you to his eternal glory in Christ, will himself restore, support, strengthen, and establish you."

It's a given, in other words, that from time to time, or even most of the time, our cups will overflow with trouble.

But our eternal God, in his eternal mercy, will use that trouble to restore and support and strengthen and establish us. Even as we walk through the dark shadows, even in the presence of our enemies, our cup will overflow with his goodness and mercy.

I believe it.

I have seen it, even in the midst of the worst four years of my life. I have seen it in my own circumstances and in the lives of so many whose faith and courage and trust inspire me.

And now, when the clouds seem to be lifting and the colors begin to shine through the clouds (but who knows what will happen in the future?), I can see so much more clearly the ways in which I have indeed been restored, supported, strengthened, and established. It didn't happen exactly the way I thought it would, but the results were so much deeper and more wonderful than I could imagine.

I really never thought it all would happen to me.

Neither did you.

But you and I could never know the wonderful things that God has in store for us when we bring him our overflowing cup of trouble, let him empty the pain, and then let him fill us to overflowing with his love.

It's Too Much, Lord!

Some Words for When Your
Cup Overflows with Trouble . . .

Even though I walk
through the valley of the shadow of death,
I will fear no evil,
for you are with me: . . .
You prepare a table before me
in the presence of my enemies.
You anoint my head with oil;
my cup overflows.
Surely goodness and love will follow me
all the days of my life,
and I will dwell in the house of the Lord
forever.

Psalm 23:4-6

Be merciful to me, O Lord, for I am in distress;
my eyes grow weak with sorrow,
my soul and my body with grief.
My life is consumed by anguish
and my years by groaning;
my strength fails because of my affliction,
and my bones grow weak.

Psalm 31: 9,10

Save me, O God,
for the waters have come up to my neck.
I sink in the miry depths,
where there is no foothold.
I have come into the deep waters;
the floods engulf me. . . .

Do not let the floodwaters engulf me
  or the depths swallow me up
  or the pit close its mouth over me.
Answer me, O Lord, out of the goodness of your love;
  in your great mercy turn to me.

Psalm 69:1,2,15,16

Dear friends, do not be surprised at the painful trial you are
suffering, as though something strange were happening to
you. But rejoice that you participate in the sufferings of
Christ, so that you may be overjoyed when his glory is
revealed.

I Peter 4:12,13

I have told you these things, so that in me you may have
peace. In this world you will have trouble. But take heart! I
have overcome the world.

John 16:33

Fear not, for I have redeemed you;
  I have summoned you by name; you are mine.
When you pass through the waters,
  I will be with you;
and when you pass through the rivers,
  they will not sweep over you.
When you walk through the fire,
  you will not be burned;
  the flames will not set you ablaze.
For I am the Lord, your God,
  the Holy One of Israel, your Savior.

Isaiah 43:1-3

Consider it pure joy, my brothers, whenever you face trials
of many kinds, because you know that the testing of your
faith develops perseverance. Perseverance must finish
its work so that you may be mature and complete, not
lacking anything.

James 1:2-4

I Rely On You

When the weight is much too hard to bear,
When it seems that I can't carry on,
Oh Lord, when all my strength is through,
I rely on you.

When I'm given over to despair,
Give me strength to come to you in prayer,
Jesus, you bring me hope anew.
I rely on you.

I rely on you, I rely on you.
My earthly strength alone will never do.
I rely on you,

I rely on you, I rely on you.
By your power, Lord, I know I'll make it through.
I rely on you.

Glenn Baxley and Michael Beaman

How Much Longer, Lord?

How much longer, Lord?
It seems like it's been too long.
I've waited and I've watched,
I've tried to be faithful.
I've tried to obey.
And let's be honest, God:
Things just aren't getting any better.
How much longer, Lord,
will I have to wait?

2

How Much Longer, Lord?

What God Did While I Was Waiting

*"And after you have suffered
for a little while . . ."*
—I Peter 5:10

$\mathcal{I}$ thought it would take three months.

I thought it would transform my daughter's life.

And I was right on both counts, except that it didn't happen at all the way I thought.

The way it did happen, though, taught me some important things about prayer . . . and waiting.

When my daughter Jenny first walked out on her husband and her marriage and her God in February of 1994, I was distraught. I was furious at Jenny for leaving. I was desperately worried for my daughter's three children. I ached for my son-in-law and worried for my husband's health as I saw him agonize over the situation.

But what could I do? How could I help?

That month, I was scheduled to speak at the Southern California Woman's Retreat. Reluctantly, and without giving any details, I shared a little of my pain and worry with the women at that retreat. And afterwards, a woman came up to me and said, "I know a book that can help you." She said, "I've had difficulties with my daughter, too. But then I found this little book called *Praying God's Will for My Daughter*. It's really Scripture arranged into topics, and it can help you to pray God's Word over your daughter. I did that, and in three months my daughter's life began to change."

"That sounds really good to me," I said. I've always believed in disciplined, focused prayer, and this book sounded like just what I needed. I really wanted God's will for Jenny. I was positive that the reuniting of that family was God's will! And three months—that wasn't so long to change a person's life. I could do this for Jenny. I *wanted* to do it.

So I went to a Christian bookstore and found the little book the woman had mentioned, *Praying God's Will for My Daughter* by Lee Roberts. In the front of the book was this promise:

> If you follow a systematic plan of praying
> God's will for your daughter, you will see
> dynamic growth take place in her life. She will
> become the person God intended her to be.

In my heart, that's what I wanted most of all. I
brought that little book home and began to think
about how I could use it.

Now, my time is pretty limited, especially with my
speaking schedule. I didn't want to give up my fifteen
minutes alone with God in my prayer closet every
morning. So I decided to take that little book along
with me to the canal path where I take my daily walk.

I like to walk two miles a day. That takes about
forty-five minutes. So I made up my mind that I
would use my walking time to pray God's Word over
my daughter using the little book I had just bought.

The day I began, I marked the date in the front of
the book. I started at the beginning, with the topic of
anger, and I prayed from Ephesians as it directed:

> God, in accordance with Your Word, I pray
> that Jenny will let all bitterness, wrath, anger,
> clamor, and evil speaking be put away from her,
> with all malice. I pray also that she will be kind
> to others, tenderhearted, forgiving others, just
> as God in Christ forgave her.

That was the beginning.

Each day I would lace up my tennis shoes, drive
to the canal path, walk, and read from that little

Scripture book. Each day I would cry, and cry to God, on behalf of my confused, hurting daughter.

Weeks passed. I worked my way from the topics of "Anger" and "Attitude" all the way through to "Worried." I reached the end of the book. Nothing had changed.

Some things take time, I reminded myself.

So I wrote the date in the back of the book and started over.

Three months had passed. The woman at the retreat had said her daughter was changed in three months, but nothing seemed different about our Jenny. She was still angry, still alienated from church, still dating men who were no good for her, still not paying enough attention (as I saw it) to her children. She showed no signs of repenting for her actions or returning to her husband.

Oh well, I sighed. *I guess God has a little harder job to do on my daughter than on this other lady's daughter!*

So I kept on walking and praying. I wrote another "finished" date in the back of the book, and then another. And one day I happened to look at those dates and I realized I had been praying God's Word over Jenny for an entire year!

That day I had been reading the Scriptures under the topic of "Trust." And as I pondered God's words on trust I suddenly realized I was weeping.

"God, I *have* trusted you," I blurted out, "and you're not *doing* anything; nothing is happening. I don't see any change in Jenny. I don't see that she's back with Craig. I trusted you for the healing of this family, I've prayed for that, and it just hasn't happened."

I stalked on down the path, pumping my arms hard in my frustration. I walked another quarter mile, then another. And then, in the depths of my heart, I seemed to hear God's answer:

Emilie, trust me, he whispered in my heart. *I know the beginning from the end.*

"God, I'm *trying* to trust you," I shot back, "but you're not making it easy! You haven't *done* anything."

And still I seemed to hear, echoing deeply: *Trust me, trust me, trust me.*

So I walked a little further, reached the end of the path, and quietly headed for my car. I finally shrugged my shoulders and said, "All right, God, I want to trust you, but you've got to help me."

So I kept up my routine of walking and praying for Jenny from that little Scripture book. But now, in addition, whenever I would think about the situation during the day, I would pray, "God, I want to trust you. Please help me to trust you."

The situation still didn't change. I worked my way through the little book again, and again. But gradually, over time, I realized I was finding it a little easier to trust God for my daughter . . . and then even a little easier.

Something was changing, *something*, although it wasn't what I wanted in the first place. Quietly, gently, my faith was growing.

Another six months passed, then another three. One day I was reading in the section on forgiveness and praying, as I often did, that I would be able to forgive Jenny for what she had done to our family. In the past weeks, God had been showing me just how angry I was with her for hurting us all with her actions.

"Dear Lord," I prayed. "I know you want me to forgive her. Please help."

And then I was surprised to hear God saying in my heart: *Emilie, you need to ask Jenny to forgive you.*

That stopped me cold. "Ask her forgiveness for what? What have *I* done to *her*? She's the one who walked out on her family."

But then as I went on to read those Scriptures on forgiveness, I began to see the answers. I also realized that I really did want to be obedient to God. And so that afternoon I called my daughter and said, "Jenny, I need to come over and talk to you."

Now, Jenny knew I had been praying the Word of God over her. So she was not really surprised when I told her what I had been reading. But she was very surprised when I said, "Jenny, please, will you forgive me? I've resented you. I've blamed you. I've been critical of you. And I'm sorry. Please forgive me for what I've said and done."

Then I left. Jenny hardly said anything—I suppose she was in shock! But two days later I received a lovely note that said, "Mom, I love you. And I do forgive you."

It was only after that that I began to see the little changes in my Jenny's life. I began to see her Bible come out. Then, all of a sudden, she was going to church again, and she took the children on the weekends when they were with her. She was talking with them and communicating better. She was going to a counselor and getting some help with her own needs. Things were definitely getting better.

But Jenny still didn't go back to her husband. She didn't want to even think about it. My grandchildren still suffered from their broken home.

And then one day as I was walking and praying, I came to the Scripture that says we're to be thankful in all things. I thought I heard God saying: *Emilie, I want you to thank me.*

And I said, "Lord, I really am thankful for the changes I'm seeing in Jenny. So thank you."

Then the Lord spoke again in my heart: *I want you to thank me for all of it.*

"But how can I do that, Lord? How can I be thankful for the pain or the separation? (At this point, no one had filed for divorce.) How can I be thankful that my precious grandchildren's hearts are broken?"

And the answer came: *I want you to thank me today for what I will do tomorrow.*

I shook my head. I honestly didn't think I could do it. I felt like a hypocrite even trying. But I still wanted to be obedient to God, and so I did begin to thank him—for what had happened in the past, for what was happening at present, for what would happen in the future.

By this time, though, nearly three years had passed by since the time I had begun praying God's Word over Jenny. And now, gradually, I was beginning to see what God had been doing all this time.

You see, I was praying for God to change Jenny.

But what God was really doing was changing *me.*

Day after day, step by step, through the Scripture-prayers I had been reading on Jenny's behalf, God had been pouring his heart into mine. Step by step, word by word, I was being restored and supported and strengthened and established, being given what I would need not only to support my family, but also to face the ongoing health problems that were now beginning to reach a crisis level in my life.

Trust me, he had said. And I was learning to trust that God was in charge and would accomplish what needed to be accomplished.

Forgive and be forgiven, he had said. And I was seeing vivid confirmation of what a dramatic change forgiveness could bring about.

Thank me, he had said. And my dutiful thanks were beginning to be heartfelt thanks . . . even for the new trials I was going through.

I didn't stop walking and praying for my daughter. In my heart, day by day, I could feel the trust and the forgiveness and the gratitude growing.

And then one day in October, after I had been praying for my Jenny more than three and a half years, I answered my phone to hear her crying hysterically. "Mom, I need you right now," she said. I live only a few miles away, and so I was soon at her door.

Her face was still streaked with tears as she led me to a chair. "Mom," she said, "I've been battling with God for three days now. And I've been reading the Word of God over and over and over again. And I truly believe God is telling me to go back home to Craig. I think I'm supposed to do whatever it takes . . . counseling, marriage therapy, whatever . . . to make it work."

And then she said, "Mom, I really want to be obedient to God, so I'm going to do that."

I was stunned and amazed. By this time, Jenny had been dating someone steadily, a good man she really loved. Her husband also had a girlfriend. The divorce papers had been filed. Jenny had gone to a counselor and worked hard on beginning a new life. And now she was telling me that being obedient to God was more important to her than this new life she was starting.

Now I really had something to be thankful for. To see my child growing in love and obedience to her heavenly Father—that was all I had ever truly wanted for her. That afternoon she and I cried together and prayed together and read the Word together. And a day or two later she went to her husband and asked him to forgive her and promised to do whatever it took to make their family whole again.

I wish I could tell you that Jenny's husband welcomed her with open arms and that their family is back together again.

Sadly, it didn't happen that way.

Rather than taking Jenny back when she asked, her husband said it was too late. He was already involved with someone else. He couldn't put the hurt behind him. He had no interest in rebuilding their relationship.

And so the actual, physical ending to this story has not been what I wanted it to be, or at least it hasn't happened yet. But the words in the front of that little book of Scripture have indeed come true. In the past year I *have* seen dynamic growth in my daughter's life. I have seen her move closer to being the person God intended her to be. God is doing a strengthening, healing, miraculous work in our lives. When I visit her home and see her praying with the children and reaching out to her neighbors, I marvel at the strong woman of God she has become.

And it all took so much longer than I expected, but that was a mercy, too. The longer I had to wait for God's answer, you see, the more I poured the Word of God into my cup.

And now, more than ever, I understand why it sometimes seems to take so long for God to accomplish his work in us.

He doesn't have to do things the long way! God is God, and if he wants to zap us with a lightning bolt, he can. He could change our circumstances with the blink of an eye. But I think God is a lot more interested in changing hearts than he is in changing circumstances. And changing a stubborn human heart takes time, even for a sovereign Lord.

And there's another reason I believe God sometimes makes us wait a bit before our prayers are answered and our pain is eased and our dreams come to fruition. So much of the time, God is planning to do so much more with our prayers and our lives than we could ever have envisioned. God sees the big picture, the whole tapestry of the way our lives intertwine with others. Much of the time, when we feel the waiting is intolerable, I believe the Lord of all is making connections and preparing us for the time when we will receive more than we ever asked for.

This has certainly been the case in my prayers for Jenny. For so long, I prayed for things to go back to the way they were. Instead, God has done a beautiful, unexpected work in all our lives. He has given me, in many ways, a new daughter.

I saw a similar, unexpectedly wonderful outworking of God's plan recently. While speaking in northern California, Bob and I became reacquainted with a couple we had known years ago in our church. When we first met them, Kyle and Jeannie had been married eight years. And although they were happy in their jobs (she's a nurse, he's a junior-high basketball coach and an assistant principal), what they wanted more than anything else was a family of their own. But it just wasn't happening. As far as any of us could tell, our prayers for Kyle and Jeannie to have a child were just going unanswered.

By the time Kyle and Jeannie received a job offer in the north and decided to move, they had also decided to try a different path to a family. Not long after their move, we received the news that they had decided to adopt. And instead of adopting an infant, they adopted two little brothers, ages five and seven, who had been in foster homes for years.

Since then, our friends have kept us informed about how their family is doing. The path has not always been smooth! Not surprisingly, those little boys came to Kyle and Jeannie with considerable emotional problems. They had never been taught discipline or manners, and they certainly did not know Christ. The family still struggles to make up for those early years of pain and neglect. But still, the lives of all four are so much better now than any of them ever dreamed.

Kyle and Jeannie wanted a baby. What they got was the chance to change the lives of two children who needed them desperately.

Those two little boys needed a home. What they got was a mother who was a nurse and could attend to their physical problems, plus an educator father who understood little boys and their needs. Today the boys are in school, and they're learning to work on computers. They can set the table and eat with manners. Best of all, they love Jesus and know the Lord's healing presence in their lives.

What a beautiful, beautiful answer to those prayers we had prayed over those long years—a loving, Christ-centered family, lovingly prepared by our heavenly Father who saw the big picture when all that most of us could see was "Wait."

I hope I can remember that the next time I hear my teeth grinding because God is taking so long to answer my prayers, when I'm ready for results and the only answer I seem to get is "Not yet."

I hope I can remember to trust . . . because God knows the end from the beginning.

I hope I can remember to keep on forgiving and asking forgiveness, even when I don't feel like doing it . . . because forgiveness is one of God's most useful tools for changing lives.

I hope I remember to thank him today for what will happen tomorrow . . . because thankfulness keeps my heart hopeful and open to receiving his blessings.

When my cup is overflowing with trouble and God doesn't seem to be doing anything, I hope I can remember that sometimes the waiting (and the growing) is exactly what I need the most.

How Much Longer, Lord?

Some Words for When Your Patience Fades . . .

How long, O Lord? Will you forget me forever?
How long will you hide your face from me?
How long must I wrestle with my thoughts
and every day have sorrow in my heart?
How long will my enemy triumph over me?
Look on me and answer, O Lord my God.
Give light to my eyes, or I will sleep in death;
my enemy will say, "I have overcome him,"
and my foes will rejoice when I fall.
But I trust in your unfailing love;
my heart rejoices in your salvation.
I will sing to the Lord,
for he has been good to me.

Psalm 13

I wait for the Lord, my soul waits,
and in his word I put my hope.
My soul waits for the Lord
more than watchmen wait for the morning,
more than watchmen wait for the morning.

Psalm 130:5,6

I waited patiently for the Lord;
he turned to me and heard my cry.
He lifted me out of the slimy pit,
out of the mud and mire;

he set my feet on a rock
   and gave me a firm place to stand.
He put a new song in my mouth,
   a hymn of praise to our God.
Many will see and fear
   and put their trust in the Lord.

Psalm 40:1-3

Be patient, then, brothers, until the Lord's coming. See
how the farmer waits for the land to yield its valuable crop
and how patient he is for the autumn and spring rains.
You too, be patient and stand firm, because the Lord's
coming is near.

James 5:7,8

In this you greatly rejoice, though now for a little while you
may have had to suffer grief in all kinds of trials. These have
come so that your faith—of greater worth than gold, which
perishes even though refined by fire—may be proved genuine
and may result in praise, glory, and honor when Jesus Christ
is revealed. Though you have not seen him, you love him; and
even though you do not see him now, you believe in him and
are filled with an inexpressible and glorious joy, for you are
receiving the goal of your faith, the salvation of your souls.

I Peter 1:6-9

You will keep in perfect peace
   him whose mind is steadfast,
   because he trusts in you.
Trust in the Lord forever,
   for the Lord, the Lord, is the Rock eternal.

Isaiah 26:3,4

Are You There, Lord?

Are you there, Lord?
I've loved you,
I've believed in you,
But right now I just really need you.
Right now,
when I'm hurting,
what I need most of all
Is to be cradled
in your everlasting arms.
Are you there, Lord?
I need you!

3

Are You There, Lord?

What I've Learned That I Already Knew

. . . the God of all grace . . .
—I Peter 5:10

*T*here's something about pain that brings us down to basics—the basics of who we are, what we can trust, and what is truly important.

When your energy is limited, extraneous matters seem, well . . . extraneous.

When you're struggling just to take another step, vital realities loom large.

There's nothing like suffering to make a person throw out what doesn't work and cling desperately to what proves real and true.

And the one reality that stared me in the face when I was hurting the most was that I needed my heavenly Father to be near.

When I was at my lowest point, when pain was wracking my body and fear was overwhelming my soul, all I could do was lie on the floor of our guest room and cry for what I needed most.

If I close my eyes, I can be there still, my cheek pressed against the braided rug, my body thin and weak and exhausted, my mind fearful and confused, my spirit drained.

"Help me, God," I whimpered.

Help me. Help me.

Help.

There were no weighty theological issues to hash out at that point. My heart cry was that of a tiny child:

I need.

And when I cried out in my most elemental need, when I was hurting too much even to pray, God was there.

I remember that bare-bones knowledge, too, that unmistakable sense that I was not alone, that my heavenly Father was suffering right alongside me, wrapping me in loving, unseen, everlasting arms.

I didn't really feel any better—not physically . . . I was still weak and thin and exhausted.

But I was also surprisingly peaceful—comforted by being so sure of this vital and life-giving reality:

God is there.

God loves me and suffers with me.

God can and will provide what I need.

One of the reasons, in fact, that I can honestly give thanks for the pain I have gone through is that in the starkness of my pain I felt God's nearness most unmistakably.

If for no other reason, I am grateful for the long rainy season in my life because it enabled me to truly *know* what I already knew.

I'm not saying I doubted these things before, although I think many of us, much of the time, are closer to practical unbelief than we would like to admit. We all forget so quickly. We all push our faith so easily to the sidelines of our lives and to the backs of our minds.

And sometimes it takes a time of testing to confirm in our hearts and our gut what we have long ago accepted with our minds.

That is what has happened to me over and over during the last four years.

In one sense, I haven't really learned much that is new, although there have been some surprises. My beliefs are not all that different than they were before Jenny left her husband, before my long, weary fight with bronchitis, before I was diagnosed with leukemia, before that excruciating ulcer pain.

But in another sense everything is new, for today I "know what I know" at a deeper, richer level than I ever thought possible.

The cup of my life is still an earthen vessel, prone to leaks, sometimes overfull with bitterness and doubt and fear and resentment, still in need of being emptied and then refilled by God.

But now, somehow, it feels like a deeper cup, a stronger cup. And when I persist in surrendering it to my heavenly Father, it seems to bubble and brim and overflow with more and more of the Lord's goodness.

During those dark years when my cup overflowed with trouble, I learned more and more of what I already knew, because God was teaching me more and more about myself . . . and about him. The result is more confidence, more faith, more commitment to ministry, more sensitivity to those I encounter in my daily walk.

What then were these long-cherished, newly discovered truths?

The first, the most important, is that God is God.

I'm not trying to be facetious here. This very basic reality, that God is the one in charge of the universe, has been one of the hardest realities for me to accept.

Like many other adult children of alcoholics (my father), I've always had a strong need to control my surroundings, to keep chaos at bay by the very strength of my energy and will. And I've really been pretty good at this for a long time. Surely it's no accident that I gravitated toward a career in teaching home and life organization!

I love to have the details of my life under control. I love to take care of myself and not be dependent on too many people. I like to keep my feelings under control, too, "stuffing" down bad feelings to the place where I don't even know they're there.

But there's nothing like a dose of rainy reality to remind even an organizational expert just how limited our control really is.

After all, I've always devoted my best energies to raising strong, godly children and nurturing a healthy family. I've insisted on family dinners and family gatherings. I've taught my children what is right. But no matter how I tried, I couldn't manage to prevent the rift in my daughter's family.

I've always placed great emphasis on healthy eating and exercise and preventative medicine. In fact, I've taken a lot of good-natured ribbing about my taste for "rabbit food." Though I believe my healthy lifestyle may actually have saved my life, I still couldn't prevent this ongoing illness that has shaken my world like a southern California earthquake.

I've always prided myself on meeting my obligations, meeting deadlines, doing what I said I would do. I take my promises seriously. But I could not control the ulcer attack that put me in the hospital and forced Bob to cancel seven consecutive seminars.

In recent years, more deeply than ever before in my life, I have had to face up to the limits of what I can do. I can't heal my own body. I can't prevent bad things from happening to the people I love. I can't keep myself from failing in sometimes minor, sometimes spectacular ways.

And the deeper that realization becomes, the more vital it becomes that I learn to turn it all over to the one who really is in control of the past, the present, and the future.

My heavenly Father is the one who truly knows the end from the beginning. He is the one who can heal my body and take care of my loved ones and make me into the person he has in mind. He is the one who sees the entire picture and makes beauty out of brokenness.

He and only he can fill my cup to overflowing with good things.

Obviously, that doesn't mean I shouldn't take my responsibilities seriously. It doesn't mean I shouldn't try to meet my obligations or take care of my body or help my family. But there's a big difference between doing my part and doing what God gives me to do . . . and assuming that it's all up to me.

I suppose it will always be a challenge to come up with just the right balance of doing what I can and turning it all over to my heavenly Father. But my experience with an overflowing cup has taught me at a deeper level than ever just who I am . . . and who God is.

God is God—the Lord of the Universe, the Maker of Heaven and Earth, my caring heavenly Father.

And I am just me. Not the Boss. Not the one in charge of making it all happen. My most important job is to surrender my cup to him, to wait on him and trust him and obey him and thank him.

So that is one of the things I've learned that I already knew. But there have been other important lessons as well.

I've realized more deeply than ever before, for example, that the disciplines of prayer and spiritual preparation are never wasted.

As my time of suffering has pushed me toward the basic realities of life, I have looked back with some regret. I've wasted my time at quite a few pursuits that now seem trivial and pointless.

But I've never regretted the time I've spent in prayer.

I've never regretted the time I've spent in God's Word.

I've never regretted the effort Bob and I put into raising our children in the Lord and teaching them right from wrong.

And I've never for a moment regretted the energy I put into nurturing relationships.

These earlier efforts, in fact, have been treasures laid up in heaven for Bob and me, provisions that God has used to sustain us and help us grow during these years of difficulty.

The habit of turning to my heavenly Father has kept the path open for me to receive his mercy.

The Scripture I studied and learned through years of Sunday school, Bible studies, and personal searching has returned to my mind again and again, supporting and encouraging me when I had no strength left for further study.

The training we gave our children has come to fruition as each of them has reached a point where they turned to God in their own pain and let him grow and mature them—then stepped willingly into the role of caring for me in my need. Even in the midst of my deepest pain, I have had this joy of watching the seeds I helped plant so many years ago grow to fruition in the lives of my children . . . and sprout beautifully in their children as well.

All this has taken some time, and our children have gone through their own times of testing. They have made their own decisions and hammered out their own relationships with the Lord. And yet I have seen so many ways that God has used Brad and Jenny's early memories and habits to bring them back to him. Over and over again, I have rejoiced that we made the effort to give them that foundation.

I rejoice, too, in the relationships I have taken the time to nurture over the years. So many dear brothers and sisters in Christ—old friends, people who have attended my seminars, publishing colleagues, church friends—have prayed for me. So many have sent me notes of encouragement without even expecting an answer. Loving friends have cajoled me into taking better care of myself, have rubbed my feet and my back, and have covered for me when I wasn't up to doing what I had to do.

Our dear friends Donna and David Otto even flew out, at their own expense, to help us put on one of my big holiday seminars. And they weren't just lending moral support. They were carrying boxes, stacking books, cooking meals . . . doing whatever they could to love us in practical, supportive ways. What a bountiful return that was on our friendship investment!

And my dear, beloved Bob, the love of my life, has been my rock, my encourager, my support. It is he who has taken the brunt of the pressure and the worry, who has fielded hundreds of phone calls, who has pitched in to cook and clean, who has handled the bills and figured out what to do with the boxes of materials from canceled seminars that just wouldn't fit into our storage areas. He's done all this on top of the stress of worrying about Jenny, worrying about me, and maintaining his own ongoing ministry.

I have no doubts that God would have supported and sustained me even if I had only come to know him after the first big rains began in my life. It is a mark of his grace that it is never too late to come to him.

And yet, what a blessing this stored-up treasure of Scripture and prayer and family and friendship has proven to be. How much firmer my faith is now, because my experience in a time of trouble has served to reinforce a faith that was already growing through these disciplines.

God can save us all no matter what we've done before.

But I know now more firmly than I ever did before that none of the disciplines of faith and obedience and love is ever wasted.

Here's another thing I've learned that I already knew: God is more interested in our inside than our outside, more concerned with our hearts than with our circumstances.

Our circumstances, in fact, are really only tools he uses to bring us to him, and he doesn't always use those circumstances the way we expect.

We human beings are always prone to focus on outer realities and forget what's happening inside. Even religious people are guilty of this, perhaps *especially* guilty of this. We focus on whether people do the right thing rather than on where their hearts are.

But that kind of thinking is exactly what led Jesus to accuse the Pharisees of being whited sepulchers— spruced-up containers for rotten bones.

God looks on the heart, the Bible tells us. He cares about our motivations, our attitudes, our relationship with him. He cares more about where we're going than about what we've done.

That doesn't mean that what we do makes no difference! Inevitably, our deeds will reflect our hearts, so what's inside is bound to come out eventually. What we do has a way of affecting our thinking, too. Works and faith will always be tied tightly together.

But as I have watched my daughter grow and blossom this last year into a committed woman of God, I have been strongly reminded that God's real concern all along has been with the real Jenny, the woman inside, not on whether her lifestyle was correct or incorrect. And he was concerned with the person inside me, and Bob, and Jenny's husband, and the children. The external circumstances were just that—external.

I still believe with all my heart that God's perfect will would have been for Jenny's original family to become intact again . . . not to mention loving, supportive, communicative, strong.

And that hasn't happened, at least not yet.

Choices were made, attitudes were chosen, words were said, mistakes were perpetuated. But God was most concerned with how we could all grow closer to him in the midst of it all. Because he is God, he even used the circumstances of that awful separation to bring about healthy changes in Jenny's character.

Today, when I look at my daughter, I see a woman who is more secure in herself than she has ever been, more sure of her commitment to her family and her God. Decisions she once made to please us, she now makes to please her Lord. She has grown, she has matured, and regardless of what happens in her marriage—I am deeply proud of the person she's become.

Yes, she still struggles. She's lonely sometimes. She has questions and doubts. And yet, when I look at my daughter now, I see a deep joy in her I never saw before. God is making something infinitely beautiful out of the brokenness of her life. He is using her circumstances to change her heart.

God really is God, in other words.

God is in control.

God is more interested in the inside than the outside, and if we remain open to him, he will use whatever circumstances we encounter to bring us closer to him.

And that brings us to another truth I have learned and relearned during this difficult period. The key to letting God do something beautiful in us during our rainy seasons is keeping ourselves open to him. And that requires those same three key disciplines I rediscovered during my prayer walks.

God can and will redeem our pain if we remain open to him.

But remaining open to him requires trusting, often when we don't feel like trusting.

It requires forgiveness, both giving and receiving, and again, often when forgiving and asking forgiveness are the last things we'd rather do.

And remaining open to God requires thanking him even when we don't feel thankful, exercising our wills to praise him for what he is doing in our lives yesterday, today, and tomorrow.

Trust: we hand him our cup.

Forgiveness: we let him wash our cup clean.

Thankfulness: we praise him for the beautiful ways in which he is going to fill that cup, even when a part of us just can't believe it.

And the thing that makes it all possible, of course, especially when we're physically drained and emotionally distraught, is that we don't even have to manage trust, forgiveness, and thankfulness on our own. All that is truly necessary is for us to be willing to try . . . and ask him to do the rest.

For that is another bedrock truth that has been proven to me over and over in these times when my need has been so great.

If we remain open and willing, our God is eternally willing to give us what we need.

He will meet us where we are, accommodating our weaknesses, catering to our particularities, poking and prodding when that will help us, comforting and encouraging when that's what will do the job.

Sometimes this provision is made in gentle, subtle ways: the call of a friend, a beautiful day, a song on the radio that cuts through our hurt with a message of encouragement, the simple awareness that we are not alone.

Other times though, the provision is both creative and surprising—like the gift of my wonderful juicing machine.

It came from out of the blue, or that's how it seemed to me. But when it came, the unmistakable message to me was of God's loving and very specific care.

As part of my quest for good nutrition and natural healing, I had explored the possibilities of acquiring a juicer. I had checked out some ads and looked into some brands and talked the issue over with my health doctor. While doing a seminar in Orlando, Florida, I had even discussed the pros and cons of juicing with a sweet Christian woman I met there, Suzanne Hinn.

But I hadn't bought a juicer yet. In fact, they seemed so expensive that I was having trouble justifying such a purchase. Sure, a juice machine would be nice, but there were other ways to get the nutrients I needed.

So I was totally unprepared, therefore, when UPS brought the big box to my door. Bob cut open the flaps and we peered inside, and I was absolutely blown away by what I saw.

My new friend Suzanne had gifted me with a juicer, the same powerful (and expensive) brand I had researched. Our conversation in Florida had been brief, and I know I never *asked* her for a juicer. But somehow that dear woman had listened to my heart and followed God's leading and chosen to respond.

Bob carefully lifted the machine out of the box and set it on the counter. And all I could do was stare at it—that splendid, extravagant gift that spoke of one woman's caring and also (I recognized in my spirit) of my Father's tender and specific provision for my needs. What a loving and creative thing for my Father to do for me! (And how wonderful of Suzanne to let herself be used in such a way!)

As I have told this story, other people have told similar stories of times when God provided for their needs in such specific and personal ways that they could not help but feel his love and caring.

My editor friend, Anne, tells with awe of a time when her computer, on which she depends to do her work, crashed. She needed that computer to finish a project so she could go on a much-needed retreat that weekend, but the whole project seemed to be lost. So she prayed—feeling a little silly to be praying about a computer, but reasoning that the God of sea and sky is also the God of electronic circuits. When she was through praying, she turned on the computer and sighed with relief to see the familiar flashing message that meant the hard drive was working.

Anne finished the project, turned off the computer, and went on the retreat, which proved to be a powerful, soul-healing experience for her. When she came back, the computer was completely dead. The memory of this "miracle," so custom-tailored to her specific needs, has been enough to sustain her in many times of doubt.

Another friend, torn apart by a bitter custody battle with her ex-husband, tells a different story of God's special and specific provision. To her, the mark of God's presence lay in finding a Christian lawyer who understood her strong desire to spare her children further pain, even if that meant giving up some of her "rights." After years of wrangling with lawyers who just wanted to "duke it out" regardless of the consequences, she is convinced that finding her current lawyer was a true miracle.

I see this same kind of special provision in Jesus' gentle treatment of the disciple Thomas. You know the story. "Doubting" Thomas, overly cautious in his pain, refused to believe the Lord had risen until he was allowed to put his hands in the nail wounds of Jesus' hands. So many who read this story focus on the doubt, on Thomas' failure. But when I read that story, what I see most strongly is Jesus' gentle provision of just exactly what Thomas needed in order to draw closer to him.

Yes, Jesus chided Thomas gently for his unbelief. But then what did he do? He simply stretched out his nail-scarred hands for Thomas to touch.

"It would be easier for you if you had more faith," I hear him saying both to Thomas and to me, "but if this is what you need, you can have it."

God provides. How deeply has that reality been engraved in my soul during these "overflowing" years! We can trust our heavenly Father to see that we have exactly what we need to grow, to thrive, to have joy.

This is not to say, of course, that our computers will always be healed and that we'll always manage to hire the best lawyer and that extravagant gifts will always arrive at our doorstep. Sometimes, in fact, we'll ask our heavenly Father for something and then discover later that he had something completely different in mind. After all, he knows our needs better than we do. And again, his eternal interest is not in our comfort, but in our growth.

But my walk through the dark shadow of a rainy season has confirmed for me again and again that I can trust my Lord to provide for my needs, whatever it takes.

He will do what he has to do to bring us closer to him.

And even more important, he will be there beside us the whole time.

Once again, that's the most basic reality my pain has brought into focus. It is the basis of my faith, the source of my trust, the foundational belief that I have had tested in a crucible of my pain and found to be true.

No matter where I go, no matter what happens, my God is always with me—suffering alongside me, working to redeem my pain, sustaining and supporting me in my weakness, shaping me into the person he wants me to be.

He is there with me on the speaking platform as I speak . . . and on the hard floor where I collapse, too weak to do anything but cry for help. He is also there when I'm better, when I turn my face to the beautiful sunshine and thank him.

God is there.

I always knew it.

But now I *know* it.

And in your own time of testing, if you keep yourself open to his working in your life, I know you will know it, too.

Are You There, Lord?

Some Words to Remind You
of What You Know . . .

Where can I go from your Spirit?
  Where can I flee from your presence?
If I go up to the heavens, you are there;
  if I make my bed in the depths, you are there.
If I rise on the wings of the dawn,
  if I settle on the far side of the sea,
even there your hand will guide me,
  your right hand will hold me fast.
If I say, "Surely the darkness will hide me
  and the light become night around me,"
even the darkness will not be dark to you;
  the night will shine like the day,
  for darkness is as light to you.

Psalm 139: 7-12

I sought the Lord, and he answered me;
  he delivered me from all my fears.
Those who look to him are radiant;
  their faces are never covered with shame.
This poor [woman] called, and the Lord heard [me];
  he saved [me] out of all [my] troubles. . . .
Taste and see that the Lord is good;
  blessed is the [woman] who takes refuge in him.

Psalm 34:4–6,8

Have I not commanded you? Be strong and courageous. Do not be terrified, do not be discouraged, for the Lord your God will be with you wherever you go.

Joshua 1:9

But we have this treasure in jars of clay to show that this all-surpassing power is from God and not from us. We are hard pressed on every side, but not crushed; perplexed, but not in despair; persecuted, but not abandoned; struck down, but not destroyed. We always carry around in our body the death of Jesus, so that the life of Jesus may also be revealed in our body. For we who are alive are always being given over to death for Jesus's sake, so that his life may be revealed in our mortal body. So then, death is at work in us, but life is at work in you. . . .

Therefore we do not lose heart. Though outwardly we are wasting away, yet inwardly we are being renewed day by day. For our light and momentary troubles are achieving for us an eternal glory that far outweighs them all. So we fix our eyes not on what is seen, but on what is unseen. For what is seen is temporary, but what is unseen is eternal.

2 Corinthians 4:7-12,16-18

The Eyes of the Lord

The eyes of the Lord are upon me, for I love him.
He will take care of my each and every need.
I'll be encouraged through hardship, I'll revere him.
I have all that I desire, for you see,
The eyes of the Lord are forever upon me.

For you are my hope when my spirit's weak.
I know you're with the brokenhearted, those who will believe.
I will trust you, for you encourage me.
I have no fear of what's ahead of me—
The eyes of the Lord are forever upon me.

Glenn Baxley and Michael Beaman

What Are You Going to Do, Lord?

What are you going to do, Lord?
I need a bit of a miracle
Right about now.
I've got these broken relationships—
And this broken body,
And these broken dreams.
And I need you to make it all better.
What are you going to do, Lord?
Can you fix this?
Will you fix this?

4

What Are You Going to Do, Lord?

Some Thoughts on Making It All Better

. . . the God of all grace . . . will
himself restore . . . you."
—I Peter 5:10

*W*hen my children (and later my grandchildren) were small, I used to delight in fixing things for them.

What a sense of satisfaction to be able to take a broken toy or a ripped shirt or a skinned knee and "make it all better" with a tube of glue or a spool of thread or a Band-Aid or just a kiss.

I also enjoyed immensely, in the days when I had a little more time and a lot less money, the process of restoring old, beat-up furniture or decorative items. With a little paint or varnish, a yard or two of fabric, and a little creative imagination, almost any worn-out item could be restored to beauty or usefulness.

I used to find such joy in my own small efforts at restoration.

So in the past few years, when I myself have felt so broken and worn, I've wondered if my heavenly Father finds the same kind of joy in restoring me.

For restoration is exactly what he promises us through Scripture.

"He restores my soul," sings the Psalmist.

"The God of all grace, who has called you to his eternal glory in Christ, will himself restore . . . you," says Peter.

In the Old Testament, God repeatedly promised his people through the prophets that he would restore the health of their nation.

Jesus, throughout his earthly ministry, restored physical health, spiritual health, even physical life . . . and passed that restorative power on to his followers through the Holy Spirit.

Even the biblical depictions of the end times are a magnificent epic of restoration, a promise to bring about a new heaven and a new earth—all fixed, redeemed, and shining good as new.

Magnificently "all better."

And that, of course, is what we all long for, especially in the rainy seasons of our lives.

When illness strikes, when experiences knock us low, when life leaves us wounded, our natural heart-cry to our heavenly Father is the cry of a child: "Please make it all better."

And he does just that. I believe it with all my heart.

How does he do it? As I see it, God has several favorite methods.

Every one of us, for example, has benefited from the normal healing processes built into creation. And these natural processes are truly miraculous.

I am astonished to see the ways that cells can regenerate to close a wound, knit a broken bone together, or combat an infection. I am amazed at the way the human mind can adapt and move forward after a disappointment or even a crushing tragedy. I am astounded by the resilience of the human spirit, the way people can rebound from a setback to live creative and positive lives.

Healing is built into the very design of the world. Scientists can study it, doctors can promote it. It is an amazing, miraculous part of life.

Unfortunately, sickness and brokenness and death are also part of life, and there's a limit to what can be fixed or healed through natural processes.

A wound can be closed, but it will leave a scar.

A broken bone can heal, but the evidence of the break will always be there for the x-ray machine to see.

The mind can adapt, the spirit can rebound, but inner wounds will leave their marks as well.

And in the physical realm, despite the miracle of normal healing, we all face one inevitable outcome: death. For all of us, eventually, the normal, natural healing processes fail.

But again, natural healing is just one of the restorative tools the Father makes use of in "making it all better."

I believe that God also works through human beings to do his restorative work. Traditional and alternative doctors can be agents of remarkable healing, and so can ministers and therapists and counselors and all those with the spiritual gift of healing. And so can loving friends who pour their energies into prayer and practical help. All these at one time or the other have been God's agents of healing in our family.

And I truly believe that, when it suits his purposes, God also intervenes directly in the natural processes he originally set in motion. I know of too many instances—either those I have directly witnessed or those told to me by people I trust, of miraculous, instantaneous healings of mind and body and spirit. I know of cases where afflicted men and women and children have literally been able to rise, take up their beds, and walk. I know of many others, when ongoing prayer occurred, whose results baffled the doctors.

(My own recent remission from leukemia falls into that category.)

And yet, I have to remember, it doesn't always happen that way. It doesn't even *usually* happen that way. Not everyone is healed suddenly and miraculously. Not everyone is even healed, at least not in the physical sense.

I know so many people who have suffered for years, faithfully praying for healing, faithfully waiting on God . . . and nothing has seemed to change.

I know of people whose rainy seasons have lasted decades, just one thing after another, with no relief in sight.

I think of the poor woman whose two daughters were afflicted with a mysterious brain lesion that rendered them all but helpless over the course of a few years. (Her radiant faith and courage inspires me.)

I think of another woman who was divorced, widowed, and afflicted with a chronic, excruciatingly painful disease, all by her early thirties. Now she is reaching the end of her childbearing years, haunted by the fact that her lifelong goal of becoming a mother may never come true. (But even as she mourns the loss of her dream, she is building a teaching and writing career that promises to change the lives of many, many children.)

I think of other friends who have struggled for years with financial difficulties, losing their homes and their businesses, and are now struggling in midlife to start over. (But in the process they have grown and matured and increased their faith—as well as building new, fulfilling careers.)

Restoration, in other words, is not always instantaneous.

Things don't always seem to get "all better" quickly.

Sometimes, in fact, they seem to get worse and worse and worse and worse.

Why? I honestly don't know the answer . . . except to tell myself once again that God is God. Our loving, redemptive, restorative Father retains the prerogative of being in charge of all things, which means that his restoration proceeds on his own timetable and according to his own priorities.

So, do I expect God to heal my leukemia, my chronic bronchitis, my ulcer? Absolutely. In the depth of my being, I expect to be healed of these things, just as I expect my heart to be healed of bitterness and fear and my spirit to be healed of rebellion and sin.

But I can't say precisely how this healing will happen.

And I can't say *when* it will happen.

Or maybe, more accurately . . . I can't say when it will be finished, because I have come to see my healing, my restoration, as an ongoing, lifelong process.

By the Lord's mercy, I am *being healed*, being made perfect, in a process that will take my entire lifetime . . . and perhaps even longer . . . to complete.

Is that cold comfort on the days that I'm aching and weary and yearning like a child to be "all better" now?

Sometimes, in all honesty, it feels that way. There *are* days when I feel my brokenness acutely and find myself whimpering, "now."

And yet there are so many other times when, even as I whimper, I can feel the gentle touch of God's comfort, soft as a mother's kiss, the quiet reminder that he is still there. Sometimes that's enough to calm me and keep me going.

And then, over the long haul, God has given me tantalizing glimpses of just how good my restoration is going to be—enough that I usually recover my trust and my patience. Again and again, I have seen him in the process of bringing beauty out of broken-ness and gently guiding his children into wholeness and maturity. How can I not trust him to finish the job in me?

Even now, I have a taste of physical restoration. With the help of God and my nutritional consultant and my other doctors and Bob and all those who have prayed for me I *am* gradually regaining my physical strength. The coughing is more or less gone. My bland ulcer diet is no longer needed. I have more energy to do my seminars and take care of my home. In general, I feel all right—a miracle in itself after so many years of feeling terrible.

I believe I have grown spiritually stronger as well: more obedient, more trusting, more passionate about following God's leading in my life. And I am watching in joy as, at the same time, my husband and my children and even my grandchildren are being spiritually restored and strengthened and my ministry is deepening and broadening.

In so many ways, my life today is better than it was before this last rainy season began in our lives. It is richer, fuller, deeper. My cup is bigger, and deeper, and truly brimming with God's goodness and mercy.

But the process is definitely not over yet.

I have no way of knowing, for example, whether my leukemia is cured or simply in remission or under control. My recent bout with stomach pain reminded me that my ulcer or the factors that caused it have not disappeared. Even on good days, I don't have the energy or the stamina that I once had.

And even if all my illnesses and discomforts were to disappear entirely, my body is still aging. There's no hiding from the fact that I'm no longer young. And one of these days, physically speaking, I'm going to die.

Similarly, I have no way of knowing whether Jenny's family will be restored to its original configuration. As I write, a divorce has been filed, but it's not yet final. My daughter has gone to her husband twice and asked to come home, saying she is willing to do what it takes for her family to be whole again. But he has not yet agreed. He might not be able or willing to get past the previous hurt. Or something else might happen to keep them all apart.

What I do know is that God is using all these circumstances to bring us closer to him (and to each other), teaching us to rely on him for our healing and restoration. And he is teaching me a lot about what it really means to be healed and restored.

I am learning, for instance, that my healing is intended to be a partnership. God does the restoration, but I am not just a passive participant. I am expected to respond and participate in the process.

I participate in the healing of my body, for instance, by following what I believe to be God's plan for a healthy life: natural nutrition, enough water, adequate exercise, enough rest. I pray for healing, and I gratefully accept the prayers of others (just as I pray for them).

At the same time, I'm trying to participate in the healing of my own soul and spirit by keeping my heart open to God, learning more about how he works, and most of all by offering him my overflowing cup and asking him to purify and restore me.

This is another thing I am learning about the process of restoration. It has a lot to do with coming clean.

My current round of physical restoration began, I believe, with the process of flushing out the toxins from my body through a program of healthy nutrition. I took my body to my nutritional consultant and she helped me begin the process of cleaning and purifying my poisoned system.

I am absolutely convinced that my spiritual restoration, as well, depends on the process of ridding my soul of spiritual toxins: stress, bitterness, resentment, rebellion, unprocessed grief, distrust. In the Bible, healing is always tied in with forgiveness of sins and cleansing of life. And I think that is absolutely true for our lives as well.

In *Fill My Cup, Lord,* I pictured this process as one of emptying our cups of these dark substances and then surrendering those cups to the Lord to be wiped clean and filled with quietness, encouragement, and forgiveness.

In our seminars we illustrate this process even more graphically, with a huge black ceramic cappuccino cup. I fill the black cup with little slips of black paper to illustrate how our cups become full of dark attitudes and emotions and thoughts and beliefs, desperately in need of a good cleaning. I urge the women to take their "cup of darkness" to the foot of the cross and dump all the blackness at his feet. (At that point I actually turn the black cup over and dump out all those little pieces of black paper.) Then I hold up another big cup, the twin of the first, except that it's gleaming white. And I ask them to picture looking into their cups and seeing them shine with white purity—unstained and unsullied, beautiful and bright and clean.

It's a simple but profound illustration. The ongoing and unending process in this life of becoming clean is one of the keys to being made "all better."

After one seminar, a woman came up to me and said, "You know, I dumped all the blackness out of my cup, and when I looked in I saw there was still something left. And I realized that I was still harboring some resentment in my heart that needs to be emptied. I'm going to go home and get my cup clean by asking forgiveness of someone."

That's exactly what we need to do to participate in our own restoration. We need to concentrate on keeping our cups clean, going to the Lord, emptying out our cups of darkness, asking to be purified and refilled. We need to stay close to him: reading the Scriptures, spending time in prayer, listening to his Word about what our part in our own healing will be.

And this is crucially important: we need to obey. Now, more than ever, I am convinced that a vital key to restoration is simply *not saying no* to God when we hear his voice.

The brokenness in our lives over Jenny's separation didn't begin to be repaired until I managed to hear God's Word about asking forgiveness and then, as hard as it was, to obey. I didn't really want to ask Jenny's forgiveness. I was still convinced she was the one in the wrong. But I didn't want to say no to God, so I did what he said. And when I asked Jenny's forgiveness, our lives began to change.

Since then I have watched with awe as Jenny has determined to participate in her own healing by obeying God. A few years ago, I saw my daughter floundering around, lashing out, confused about who she was and where she fit in her own life. Yet today I see her praying with her children, doing what she can to help them in their own pain, reaching out to her friends and the people in her new neighborhood. I've seen her close the door on more than one promising romantic relationship in the hope that her marriage can be restored. I've seen her obey God when she really didn't want to, and the result has been phenomenal growth in her life.

So we do participate in our own restoration. Through ongoing surrender and obedience, even when it's hard, we help in the process of ridding our lives of physical and emotional and spiritual toxins that are poisoning our lives and preventing our healing and growth.

And yet there always comes a point when we reach the limits of our participation. At some point we have to come back to the realization that God, once again, is in charge of how we heal and when we heal and what the end result will be. He alone is the one who can ultimately "make it all better." But that is wonderful news to me, because only in him does "all better" mean perfect, fully whole, and better than new.

In this life, almost all healing leaves scars behind, visual testimonies to our wounds and our illnesses and our failings. Like the shattered teacups I once glued together after a shelf collapsed, the repairs will show. We may be restored, but we're not really as good as new.

But one day, we are promised, if we remain in him, our Lord will make us better than new: completely redeemed, remade, more beautiful than we ever imagined, with no seams, no scars, no Band-Aids, no patches.

It's a little like Margery Williams' beautiful little story of *The Velveteen Rabbit.* No doubt you have read this beloved children's book about the little stuffed rabbit who wanted to be real. This toy rabbit was loved by his young owner until his velveteen fur was worn and his face was gone and his stuffing was coming out. But somehow, in the process of being loved to tatters, this little toy bunny was given the gift of becoming "real."

The point of the story, of course, was that we become real by loving and being loved, but that in the process we get hurt and collect some scars.

But I think the ending of that beautiful little story makes another point as well.

In his first life the velveteen rabbit was a stuffed toy covered with scars.

By the end of the story, though, he was not just repaired. He wasn't just patched up, glued together, fixed up.

Instead, the velveteen rabbit was transformed, made new, still fully himself but at the same time fully new. He wasn't a patched-up toy bunny. He was a beautiful, bounding, real rabbit, set free by love to explore an entirely new world.

And that's the kind of healing I look forward to eventually, when I'm through with this life and ready for my new life in the Lord.

Here on earth, the restoration we experience is an ongoing process, truly miraculous but partial and problematic. Here on earth, the very process of healing leaves us inevitably marked and scarred (not to mention wrinkled and sagging).

In the end, though, the healing we are promised is full and complete. When God is through with us, we will be more real than we ever thought possible—as well as unscarred and unwrinkled and energetic and full of life and love.

I don't know about you, but I just can't wait!

What Are You Going to Do, Lord?

Some Words to Help
Restore Your Soul. . . .

For there is hope for a tree,
If it is cut down, that it will sprout again,
And that its tender shoots will not cease.

Job 14:7 NKJV

O Lord my God, I called to you for help
    and you healed me.
O Lord, you brought me up from the grave;
    you spared me from going down into the pit.
Sing to the Lord, you saints of his;
    praise his holy name.
For his anger lasts only a moment,
    but his favor lasts a lifetime;
weeping may remain for a night,
but rejoicing comes in the morning.

Psalm 30:2-5

Create in me a pure heart, O God,
    and renew a steadfast spirit within me.
Do not cast me from your presence
    or take your Holy Spirit from me.
Restore to me the joy of your salvation
    and grant me a willing spirit, to sustain me.

Psalm 51:10-12

You restored me to health
   and let me live.
Surely it was for my benefit
   that I suffered such anguish.
In your love you kept me
   from the pit of destruction;
you have put all my sins
   behind your back.

Isaiah 38:16,17

But those who wait on the Lord
Shall renew their strength;
They shall mount up with wings like eagles,
They shall run and not be weary,
They shall walk and not faint.

Isaiah 40:31 NKJV

Therefore you shall be perfect, just as your Father in heaven
is perfect.

Matthew 5:48 NKJV

I Can't Do It, Lord!

I can't do it, Lord!
I don't like to admit that, but it's true.
I've never felt so weak, so helpless,
so unlikely to succeed.
I need help, Lord.
But I'm so used to taking care of myself,
I'm not even sure how to be helped.
I've always let people lean on me.
But I've never really learned how
to lean on anyone.
I can't do it, Lord . . . but you can!
Help me learn to accept the help
you give me
and, leaning,
to take one more step.

5

I Can't Do It, Lord!

The Joy of Learning to Lean

. . . the God of all grace . . . will
himself support, strengthen . . . you."
—I Peter 5:10

I've always been a can-do kind of person.
Practical, energetic, organized, determined, I'm the
sort you want on your committee, on your team. I
manage my time well. I keep my deadlines. I keep my
commitments.

I can.

I can.

Until recently, when I found myself saying, over
and over, "I can't. I just can't."

"Not again," I told Bob after more than one
draining seminar. "I just can't get on another plane
or another platform."

"Not this year," I said, shaking my head as another
Christmas drew near and we faced the annual task,

usually well loved, of decorating our house and grounds. "This year I can't even put up a tree."

"I just can't entertain you here," I told a colleague who usually stayed at our house as we worked together. And I *love* entertaining.

"I just can't get up again," I sobbed to God more than once during my weakest time. "I can't even pray to you!"

I can't.

I can't.

I could barely stand to say the words.

Though honest and true, they were a painful blow to my entire sense of who I am.

If you're a can-do person . . . what happens when you *can't* do?

I know the answer to that question now, though it took me several painful years.

When you reach the point where you simply can't, you find help. You ask for help if you need it, and you accept help when it's offered. You learn to lean on your family, your friends, your brothers and sisters in Christ, and especially on your Lord.

In the process, you receive a precious gift that is so much greater than the intrinsic value of the services given . . . and you give a wonderful gift as well.

You receive the priceless gift of realizing how much you are loved and cared for. More valuable still, though not often as pleasant, you receive the gift of recognizing your own humanness, your own weakness. You come to more realistic terms with who you are and who God is.

And at the same time, you *give* others the joy and satisfaction of serving you. That's a gift I've always truly appreciated as a "can do" person.

It's taken me a long time to realize it, but learning to lean has been one of the most valuable lessons of this rainy season in my life.

You see, leaning may not be difficult for you. But it has never come easy for me.

I grew up in a home where you couldn't always depend on others to take care of your needs—my father because he was an unpredictable alcoholic, my mother because she was abused by my father and then later, after my father died, preoccupied with trying to support us.

I learned early to take care of myself and others. And I liked the role of caretaker. I liked nurturing others, giving to others, easing their pain and their burdens, teaching them what I knew. Being strong was a comfortable role, one that felt safe to me. And I was good at it.

Now, I don't mean I was a screaming, imperious control freak. The gentle example of my mother, my satisfying marriage partnership, and even my own quieter personality kept me from that. Besides, until the last four years, I had pretty much been able to handle the difficulties life threw at me.

There were problems, of course—who doesn't have them? I've told many a seminar audience about my experience of running a household with five little children under five years old (when I myself was just twenty-one). But that kind of difficulty was right up my alley; with my natural energy and my organizational skills I quickly had that household running smoothly.

Other difficulties happened too: financial setbacks and times of unemployment, my mother's death, the sickness and death of my uncle and then my auntie, the stresses of beginning a business. These stretched me more, but they, too, proved within my capabilities. Bob and I always leaned on each other during these times, but the leaning was always more or less equal. I never reached that humbling, maddening "I can't" stage.

Then, as my emotional and then my physical weakness progressed, I began to realize I wasn't up to the tasks before me.

We had booked seminars solidly three years in advance.

We had a bustling, punishing schedule of speaking and writing and promoting our books.

We had a full life outside our work, with responsibilities to family and friends.

And, well . . . I just couldn't.

I tried. I pushed myself. I soldiered on.

I also did everything I could to take care of myself—I ate right, drank my water, and exercised daily (until that, too, became too much).

And all the while I was getting sicker and weaker.

I learned early on to depend on God's strength when it came to my speaking. I learned that when I felt too weak even to step up on a platform, the Holy Spirit would take over and give me strength. I would emerge from a seminar dazed and drained . . . but also in awe of the things God had done through me. The results I saw in those seminars—people touched and lives changed—were so clearly from the Lord and not from me . . . quite simply because there was nothing left of me to give.

As time went on and my health declined even further, I also found myself leaning more and more on Bob—first to handle more and more of the business, then increasingly to handle almost everything but the actual speaking, as well as his own ministry of speaking and writing. (On at least one occasion, when I was too ill even to get out of bed, he took over the speaking as well.) At home, there were more and more evenings when Bob was responsible for the cooking and cleaning chores I normally handled. When I ended up in the hospital with my ulcer, Bob was left with the frustrating details of canceling seminars, answering the madly ringing phone, and being at the hospital for me.

This shift of responsibility was frustrating for both of us. It was difficult for my Bob because of the sheer hard work, the worry over me, and the loss of the comforting haven I had always tried to create for us at home. It was difficult for me because I hated to see him working so hard, I felt guilty, I felt useless, and of course I felt sick.

But in the long run, this time in which I had to lean so heavily on Bob proved beneficial for both of us. It cemented our trust in each other and our gratitude for each other. And it powerfully strengthened our mutual trust in the Lord, on whom we both had to lean so heavily just to get through each day.

In the past months, as I've been feeling better and been able to look back on those dark months, I can rejoice at how God strengthened my Bob and supported him and made him wiser.

Learning to lean has not been fun for either of us, but it truly has been a gift.

Here's another gift that has emerged beautifully from those "I can't" days. After years of being strong for my children, I have had to learn to lean on them as well. In doing so, I have seen them take giant steps forward into greater maturity, and we have all received yet another gift—that subtle shifting of relationships that turns parents and children into true friends.

I will never forget the evening that Bob and I came home late from a holiday seminar to find a Christmas wreath hanging from our gate.

That was a surprise to both of us. Just a few days earlier, before we left for the seminar, I had finally confessed to Bob that I just wasn't up to decorating. This reality had darkened our spirits for the several days we had been away, because we both love the process of turning our home into a Christmas wonderland. We both knew I was right; there was no way we could manage to finish our seminar schedule and still tackle the demanding task of decorating. But we were saddened by the thought of celebrating a Christmas without the spirit-lifting magic of a decorated house.

The first thing that crossed my mind as we turned in the gate that night was that Bob had gone ahead and hung the wreath. But no, he was just as puzzled as I was.

We turned in at the gate and rounded the curve of the driveway that would take us past the trees and down to the house.

We expected it to be dark and empty. Instead, every light in the house was on.

"Is someone in the house?" I asked nervously. Cautiously we emerged from our van, tiptoed to our kitchen door, unlocked it, and pushed the door open.

Then our jaws dropped to our chins as the warm aroma of Christmas potpourri met our nostrils and the sweet sounds of Christmas carols met our ears.

We pushed the door open wider. Another giant wreath hung on the fireplace of our breakfast room. Through the island that separates the kitchen from our all-purpose great room, we could see the twinkle of little white lights entwined in mantle greenery and the glitter of a ceiling-high, beautifully decorated Christmas tree.

By now we were rushing inside like small children on Christmas morning, looking around in wide-eyed wonder.

Every room of the house was completely decorated with greenery, lights, candles, and the hundreds of ornaments we've collected over the years. There was even a second Christmas tree in the garden room, which also serves as my office. That house looked like Disneyland—a Disneyland all ready for the holidays.

It turned out that we had been visited by four very loving elves: Jenny and her three children, Christine, Chad, and Bevan. While we were gone they had come to the house, pulled out our boxes of decorations, and put them all up. They had sprayed potpourri, put Christmas music on the CD player, and then left their beautiful creation for us to find. There was even some dinner in the refrigerator, waiting to be warmed up.

That gift of caring was by far the best Christmas present either of us received that year. It brought Jenny and the children great joy as well. And it was a joy that would never have come if I hadn't reached the point of "I can't." That kind of joy is truly worth all the years of pain.

But even that beautiful memory is nothing compared to the joy we experienced on another afternoon several months later, when I was at the low point of my physical strength. That day shines among my dark memories of that time like a diamond in a mud bucket.

In those days, I couldn't see a chair or a bed or a couch without having an overpowering desire just to sit or lie down. One day I had sunk down on the big floral sofa in our great room and was just lying there, unable to move, when my Jenny walked in. She sat down beside me on that couch, took my hand, and said, "Mom, you know how much I love you, and I want you to get this sickness taken care of."

And then my Jenny prayed over me.

Now, I need to tell you that in the thirty-eight years of my daughter's life, nothing remotely like that had ever happened. Jenny had never prayed over me. To my knowledge, she had never prayed out loud as an adult—I had never heard any oral prayers from her other than "Now I Lay Me Down to Sleep." But now she was praying over me in her own words, pouring her heart out to God, asking him to strengthen and heal me. I wish now I had a tape of that beautiful prayer.

Bob, who happened to be in the kitchen, heard the prayer, too, and tears came to his eyes because he had never heard Jenny pray out loud either.

What a gift our daughter gave us both that day: the gift of her support, the gift of prayer, the gift of a love strong enough to do something she'd never dared to do before. And that gift, like so many others, grew directly out of my weakness and my need.

Not long after that, I received a phone call from our son, Brad. Now Brad lives a very, very busy life, with a demanding job and a wife who travels because of her work. When Maria is gone, he has primary responsibility for the house and their two little boys. But Brad told me, "Mom, come to my house. I'm going to take care of you. We'll take care of you here." He felt so deeply the pain I was going through; all he could think of was doing whatever he could to relieve that pain.

Tears ran down my face as I heard that tender, loving offer from my caring, sensitive son. That he was willing to make that sacrifice for me touched me deeply. Once again, I was being blessed in the midst of my weakness.

All through that season of pain I learned lessons in letting others care for me, simply because I had no choice—because I needed them, and they were pleased to fill that need.

I'll never forget a weekend seminar we had booked in Henderson, Texas. That whole weekend would be a nightmare memory were it not for the generous and thoughtful care Bob and I received from our hosts—and my heavenly Father's sustaining care as well.

This was during the time when my bronchitis was becoming chronic, when I could hardly draw a breath without my body being racked with fits of coughing. We flew into the Dallas/Fort Worth Regional Airport and rented a car, and all during that two-hour drive to Henderson, my bronchitis grew steadily worse.

We stopped first at the church where the seminar would be held and set up the facility for the next day's meeting. Then we proceeded to the home of our hosts, who live on a ranch a bit out in the country.

Usually, we prefer not to stay in private homes during a seminar. I have found that I really need the privacy of a motel or hotel in order to completely relax and build the strength I need to do my best as a speaker. But that weekend we had departed from our usual practice and agreed to stay at this lovely couple's home. Our hostess had assured us that we would have a completely private room with its own bath and a separate entrance.

It was a lovely home, and our quarters were truly wonderful; we even had our own television set. But by the time we reached the place, I could barely hold my head up, let alone appreciate the beautiful ranch setting. I was feverish and shaking, and it took everything I had just to say a friendly hello.

Our hostess immediately saw how sick I was and ordered me straight to our beautifully decorated guest quarters. There I crawled into bed and proceeded to get steadily sicker while our hosts entertained Bob, showing him around the ranch and feeding him a wonderful dinner. I was so grateful for this hospitality; their caring for Bob relieved me of that worry. From time to time our hostess would check on me as well, asking if I needed anything, but for the most part they granted me welcome privacy.

Bob finally crawled into bed about ten that evening and put his arms around me. By then I was perspiring heavily, shaking with chills, and coughing uncontrollably. I didn't see how I could possibly get out of bed the next morning, let alone speak for five hours.

But then my Bob began to pray over me. He asked God for a very specific blessing—just a window of eight hours in which I would be strong enough to speak to the women who had signed up for the conference.

Now, I respect prayer. And I believe in miracles. But I have to confess I didn't think God could do anything about this situation. Nevertheless, I sank back into Bob's arms and finally fell asleep.

The next morning I got up, and I felt better. I was able to eat a little breakfast, and then a little later I managed to get up on that platform once more and speak. It was not until we were in the car that night, returning to the airport, that the symptoms started to return. I was very sick for two weeks after that, but God had indeed granted us the eight-hour window my Bob had asked for.

From that time on, I have thought of Henderson, Texas, as a special time and place when I couldn't, but God could . . . and did. I have also thought of it as a place where I had no choice but to lean on others—our amazingly gracious hosts, whom I had never met, but who provided me with such a healing haven; and my dear Bob, who was strong for me and prayed for me when I was too sick even to pray for myself. And I think of it as a place of blessing, where I experienced intensely both the discomfort and the ultimate gift of learning to lean.

Since then, I've become even more experienced at leaning: on my family, who cared for me tenderly; on our precious friends, who visited me in the hospital and ministered to Bob and even came out to help me do seminars; on the health care professionals, who used their healing skills to make me better; on the many, many people who have written and told me they were praying for me.

During the times when I was sickest, I couldn't even summon the strength to read the hundreds of cards that came, let alone answer them, but I felt so keenly the caring and the prayer they represented.

I took to heart the reality that one woman so beautifully wrote me:

> The next time you look upon the evening sky draped in moonlight and sprinkled by stars, remember, those twinkles represent countless prayers beseeching our Lord for your recovery and renewed strength.

I have seen those stars, felt those humbling prayers, uplifting prayers, and drawn on that strength as I struggle to heal.

Now, it's possible that all these praises I'm singing of my support system have you depressed instead of encouraged. Perhaps you're thinking, *But I don't have friends like that. I don't have a husband. I don't have a family.*

But if there is one thing I have learned in this entire rainy season of our lives, it's that God will provide the support we need to get us through a time of trouble. The hard part, as I see it, is learning to ask for the support we need. Sometimes we have to take some action, to actively seek a support group.

Not long ago, in a woman's magazine, I read a very moving story of a young woman who discovered she had terminal cancer. This woman had no husband and no family at all in New York City, where she lived. But she did have friends—a disparate group who didn't even know each other. One day, not long after her diagnosis, she called six friends together and made an unusual request: would they be her family and help her through the hard months ahead?

At first they were shocked by the request, but then they felt honored, and they all agreed to help. These six women became a kind of support committee. They made sure that their friend always had someone to take her to the doctor, someone to hold her head when she was sick from the chemotherapy, someone to grocery shop and cook for her when her energy and appetite waned. They stayed with her to the end, helping her to die with grace and dignity, and in the process these women formed a powerful bond among themselves that has lasted to the present day.

What a beautiful example of graceful leaning. What a gift that woman gave herself and her friends, a creative gift that began with her courageous decision to forge a support system where there wasn't one before.

However I put together my support system, the reality holds: I come to know so much more deeply the beautiful blessings that God sends my way when I reach the point where I simply have to lean on somebody. In times like that, I am gradually learning the secret of what I always "can do."

I can cherish and appreciate the care of friends who love me.

I can luxuriate in the prayers of people who care enough to hold me up.

And I can lean on the strength of my Lord God, who has promised to be strongest when I am weak. Again and again, that promise has proved to be true.

In so many areas of my life, I am finding, I really can't.

But God can.

And maybe that's the whole point.

I Can't Do It, Lord!

Some Words to Help
You When You "Can't Do" . . .

What strength do I have, that I should still hope?
   What prospects, that I should be patient?
Do I have the strength of stone?
   Is my flesh bronze?
Do I have any power to help myself,
   Now that success has been driven from me?

Job 6:11-13

God is our refuge and strength,
   an ever-present help in trouble.
Therefore we will not fear, though the earth give way
   and the mountains fall into the heart of the sea,
though its waters roar and foam
   and the mountains quake with their surging.

Psalm 46:1-3

Do not fear, for I am with you;
   do not be dismayed, for I am your God.
I will strengthen you and help you;
   I will uphold you with my righteous right hand.

Isaiah 41:10

. . . There was given me a thorn in my flesh, a messenger of Satan, to torment me. Three times I pleaded with the Lord to take it away from me. But he said to me, "My grace is sufficient for you, for my power is made perfect in weakness." Therefore I will boast all the more gladly about my weaknesses, so that Christ's power may rest on me. That is why, for Christ's sake, I delight in weaknesses, in insults, in hardships, in persecutions, in difficulties. For when I am weak, then I am strong.

2 Corinthians 12:7-10

I urge, then, first of all, that requests, prayers, intercession and thanksgiving be made for everyone—for kings and all those in authority, that we may live peaceful and quiet lives in all godliness and holiness. This is good, and pleases God our Savior, who wants all men to be saved and to come to a knowledge of the truth.

1 Timothy 2:1-4

It's My Prayer

It's my prayer
To be filled
To overflowing,
That I may be spilled
Upon broken, hurting people everywhere—
It's my prayer.

It's my joy, Lord,
To be your humble servant
To those who are in need
Let me be the loving hand that you employ
It's my joy.

Glenn Baxley and Michael Beaman

It's All You, Lord!

It's all you, Lord!
I knew that before,
but I've had to learn it
again and again.
Without you, I am nothing—
with you, I'm one link
in a chain of blessing
That reaches round the world.
How can I say no to you?
As long as you lead
I have to follow.
It's all you, Lord.
I can't wait to see where
you'll take me next.

6

It's All You, Lord!

Links in the Blessing Chain

*. . . the God of all grace . . . will
himself establish . . . you."*
—I Peter 5:10

*I*f I'm honest, I have to admit it.

There's a part of me that would absolutely love
to hang it all up and retire.

To give up traveling, give up speaking, give up
putting books together and answering the phone and
the letters . . . I really don't think that would feel like
a hardship to me.

If I let myself, in fact, I can get lost in wonderful
daydreams of spending my weeks puttering in my
little kitchen and baking my little bread and washing
my little dishes and even cleaning my little toilet. I
love doing all that—yes, even the toilet. My happiest
times involve just snuggling down in my nest, especially when my whole family is gathered around me. I

would relish more time just to be a grammie—baking cookies with my five precious little ones, picking flowers together, going on picnics, having tea parties.

So why do I keep on?

Why don't I quit, as so many friends have been asking me to do?

"It's just too much," they say. "You need to take care of your health."

"Surely you've done enough," they say. "Maybe all the difficulties are a sign that it's time to give it up. Maybe it's time."

But I don't think so. The more I think about retiring, in fact, the more I find that I'm just not ready . . . or, more accurately, that God just isn't finished with me yet. If it were time to quit, why would my heavenly Father keep on filling my cup with compassion for these women I speak to? Week after week, even when I'm feeling weak and inadequate, I see him working through me—me! . . . to help women draw closer to him. Week after week, I find myself truly awed at the good and great things God is doing.

I see what God is doing in our lives—teaching us new things about him and confirming old truths in ways that we long to share.

I see what God is doing *through* our lives and through our ministry—somehow, amazingly using our feeble efforts to change lives. People come up and tell us how they have been touched. We receive basketloads of mail saying the same thing. (After our four years of rainy season, we are absolutely convinced that it's God who's doing the touching—not because we're reluctant to take credit, but because I just haven't been strong enough to deliver!)

How can I quit when I see God doing such wonderful, exciting things?

Now more than ever, God has given me a deep passion for the women I speak to. For me, that is the strongest reason of all to keep on going.

I *want* to be an agent of God's love to these women.

I want to be a witness for what he has done for me and what I am sure he wants to do for them—for *you*.

I want to share my hurts so they will feel liberated to share theirs.

I want to be a link in the wonderful chain of blessing I see God forging in my world. And so I'm not ready to quit, at least not yet.

Now, I am not saying that I can only be part of God's healing work by continuing my formal ministry. I really do believe I can further God's kingdom by cleaning my toilet . . . if that's what he's calling me to do. There was a time in my life when that truly was my calling.

But I believe, and Bob believes, and our family has come to believe, that God wants us right where we are at this moment. When it's time to quit, we believe, he'll show us somehow—and Bob and I will joyfully pack up our van and head for home one last time.

In the meantime, I plan to hang around for as long as God gives me strength, marveling at the beauty of what I see him doing in people's lives.

This isn't about me, remember.

I'm just one small part in what God is doing in my corner of the world. But I love to see how I fit in—how blessings given to me have multiplied manyfold in the lives of so many others.

This, in fact, is one of the greatest blessings of all.

So often in our lives, we must act only by faith, without seeing the results. We must do what we know is right, often without seeing the benefits in our lifetime.

So often, this has been true for me.

Right now, though, in this brief time of respite after so many years of onslaught, God seems to be granting me the gift of seeing results. Like Moses so long ago, I am being taken up on the mountain to see the big picture. And from here I can see the blessing chain so clearly—the blessings that have come before me and those that are still being formed, link by link, into the future.

Looking behind me, I can see so many who encouraged me, who taught me, who passed God's blessings on to me.

I think of my gentle, loving Mama. In many ways hers was a sad life, full of hard work and mistreatment by those she loved. But she was the one who laid the foundation for my ministry by teaching me both the spirit and the skills for making a home.

I think of my daddy, too. He was a tormented man, in some ways a violent man. But he passed along to me something of his fierce creativity, his passion for quality and beauty. And I think that, despite his turbulent ways that left me fearful and shy, he also gave me a special sense of being loved, of being the apple of his eye. In his own troubled way, my daddy loved me deeply, and I knew it. That sense of being special and lovable has persisted deep in my heart, laying a foundation for my happy marriage and even my acceptance of God's love.

There have been so many, many more "blessing links" who have passed along God's blessing to me and empowered me to pass it on to others.

I think especially of Florence Littauer, that gifted writer and speaker (and good friend), who gently poked and prodded me into my own ministry. She was the one who included me in her program of speakers, who taught me how to relate to an audience. She was the one who told her publisher about me and then strong-armed me into doing my first book. (Oh, my dear friend, what did you get me into?)

She and so many others encouraged me, believed in me, led me, shaped me into what I am today. They are precious links in the chain of blessing that I hope to see grow longer and longer.

And then of course, there's my Bob, who introduced me to my Savior, who has modeled Christ's love and taught me so much about living in the Lord. Where would I be without all these years of working side by side, loving each other, bearing one another's burdens, serving our Lord together?

When I married Bob, I was a seventeen-year-old Jewish schoolgirl. In the years since then he has upheld me, challenged me, encouraged me, stood firm beside me when I needed it, pushed me forward when the time was right.

This year, on our forty-second wedding anniversary, I happened to be in the hospital. I had a tube up my nose. IVs trailed from both my arms. I was perspiring profusely from my leukemia and in deep discomfort from an incision on my abdomen, the aftermath of ulcer surgery. I had not eaten in five days, and the only sustenance I could tolerate was ice chips.

In other words, I was not feeling my best or my most beautiful that evening.

But when Bob arrived in my hospital room that evening, he was dressed up for a wonderful evening out. He was wearing a tie and jacket, and he carried a box.

Confused, I just looked at him. What in the world was he doing?

He just smiled at me and opened the box. Out came a candle in a crystal holder. Out came two glasses, a plate, a pair of beautiful napkin holders, a tray, and a snowy Battenburg lace place mat with matching napkins. Finally, out came, of all things, a box of Kentucky Fried Chicken. (Bob and I share many things, but he doesn't always share my nutritional convictions.)

Tenderly, Bob filled my beautiful stemmed glass with ice chips. He poured himself some cranberry juice and arranged the chicken dinner on his plate. He lit the candle, and we toasted each other—our commitment, our love, our forty-two years of marriage. What a beautiful evening we had there in that candlelit hospital room. Never in my life has a glass of ice chips meant more to me.

In sickness and in health . . . now I can see so clearly the beauty of God's ongoing plan. For more than forty years now, our lives have been linked together—two more links on God's chain of blessing. So much of what I have been able to pass along about the Father's love and faithfulness is what Bob has given me.

Looking back, I am truly awed at the many links that have been formed by the blessing chain, right down to the link that is me. But looking forward, I am even more awed to see the way the chain stretches on and on into the future.

I see the things we taught our children (and wondered if they ever heard) now being taught and modeled for our grandchildren, each one another beautiful link in what God is preparing for the future.

I see women who tell me they've attended my seminars and felt led by God to make their homes more beautiful and welcoming sanctuaries, thus planting seeds of caring in the generations to come. I talk to women who hear my Jenny's story and are moved to go home and try to make their difficult marriages work.

I meet other women who hear my story of pain and are encouraged to tell their own stories, to God and to others, thus beginning the process of healing in their own lives. I have begun to feel that this last process is going to be one of the most important aspects of my ministry. So many people these days are in pain, and I believe that we must learn to share our pain before we can begin to be healed.

And then, there's also the music.

This ongoing tale, which began about the same time this book did, stirs my heart every time I tell it. I am absolutely astounded by the way one thing leads to another in the cycle of blessing when men and women of God, even men and women whose cups overflow with trouble, agree to be his instruments.

My part of the story begins back about the time that Jenny first left her husband. In deep pain over this rift, I suffered in silence for awhile, then gradually began to share a little of what I was going through with the women in my conferences. And as I opened up my heart to share my pain, women began to open their hearts to me. Some spoke to comfort me, to tell me that they understood and were praying for me. Others told me of their own troubles—I was stunned to see the depths of suffering that hid behind the smiling faces at my conferences. And in it all, God was working, through me and to others, to minister to all this pain.

Gradually, as I continued to speak and minister, the seeds of a little devotional book called *Fill My Cup, Lord* were sown. From the very beginning, my editor and I felt that book was special, somehow anointed. We both had a sense that God had a plan for that book far beyond our words or the beautiful package the publisher created.

We were right. Somehow that little book spoke to hurting people in a way that none of my other books had. When we sold the book at seminars, it would disappear faster than any other product. Sales figures were high. And I was receiving letters and phone calls from hundreds of women whose lives had been touched from reading that book.

What a joy! And what a blessing. Although my life was growing progressively more troubled and I was beginning to realize that something was seriously wrong with my body, I still rejoiced to see the ministry of that little book.

Not long after *Fill My Cup, Lord* was published, a young music minister in southern California was asked to compose some music for a women's retreat. Seeking inspiration, he happened to pull my little devotional off the shelf at a Christian bookstore. He read the book, liked it, composed some nice music for the retreat, and filed the book away on his own shelves.

And then, not long afterward, his life fell apart.

Due to a series of bad choices, Glenn Baxley lost his family, lost his job, lost his home, moved to another city. He was cast adrift, without moorings. At one point he was sleeping on the couch in the office of a friend's church, with no other place to go.

After a time, Glenn was reminded of *Fill My Cup, Lord* again. Somehow, through that book's message, God was pouring inspiration into the broken cup of his own life. Sitting down at a piano, he and Michael

Beaman, a talented Christian friend, composed a beautiful new song based on the title of my book—which, interestingly enough, had been taken from a song in the first place!

The new "Fill My Cup, Lord" song was just a start. God had worked another miracle by bringing Michael and Glenn together. These young men composed one beautiful song after another, each one based on a different chapter of my devotional.

Then, with their new songs in hand, Glenn and Michael connected with two enterprising men in the publishing industry—Bob Hawkins, Sr., the retired founder of Harvest House Publishers, and Rich Boyer, a talented musician and accountant. As the four of them talked, the idea was born for a series of devotional tapes combining voice-over meditation and original music.

Out of this idea a whole new company was born, Sweetwater Productions. The *Fill My Cup, Lord* tape and CD were to be its very first products.

I didn't really know this whole story until Glenn came over to my house so I could record my voice-overs for the CD. Since then, both he and Michael have become dear friends to me. We have shared our stories with one another, and we have marveled at how God has taken my original pain over Jenny's separation and produced first a new facet to my ministry, then a book that was better than anything I could ever do, then a set of songs that turned a young man's life around, and then a brand new company based on a whole new genre of devotional material. Who ever would have thought of it all?

This last Christmas, Glenn and Michael agreed to play some of their wonderful music at the big annual holiday seminar we hold at our home church, Victoria Community Church. This was not an easy decision, especially for Glenn, who is an intensely private person. But not only did they sing and play, they actually told a bit of their story and witnessed to the women in that seminar. Through God's overflowing grace, Glenn's cup was filled with a new ministry to share his testimony of how God redeemed his life back. As I saw the tears streak the eyes of the women in that seminar, I knew that yet another link had been formed in that chain of blessing that began so long before I ever wrote a book or held a seminar.

That beautiful weekend, my cup overflowed with so much beauty I could hardly contain it.

You see, the Victoria Community Church holiday seminar has always been a big family event for us. My granddaughter Christine has sung for the seminar since she was four, and the other children usually have parts as well. Jenny was involved with organizing the event and also selling T-shirts and sweatshirts she had decorated. (There's a crafts fair associated with the event.)

Wanting us all to be together, I had asked our son Brad to bring his family as well. Maria, who is a sports broadcaster, was out of town, but Brad brought his sons, Bradley Joe and Weston.

I was thankful for Brad's presence that evening. I have always had a special tenderness in my heart for this quiet, sensitive man who is so like me. And in many ways, over the past few years, my heart had been hurting for Brad as well as Jenny. For one thing, I knew that when he left home for college he stopped going to church—though I knew that in recent years he had begun to draw back to the Lord. I have also seen him struggle with the responsibilities of a high-octane career, a showplace house in Laguna Beach, and a beautiful, busy family. And I knew that he, perhaps more than anyone, had suffered with worry over my illness.

So I was thankful that Brad was there that night. I appreciated his support, and I also hoped he would receive a blessing from the Lord. But I was unprepared for the beautiful letter I received from my wonderful, sensitive son the next week:

Dear Mom,

I can't express to you how much of an impact your words had on me last weekend. As you know, I have been dedicating my life to the Lord more and more

133

over the last few months. I have asked God to work in me in ways that I've never asked for before.

The Lord's Word has been reaching me in very special ways, mainly when I'm in a church and mainly in ways that hurt. I realized I must have a lot of pain in me, because as I hear God's words they come with tears. I understand that I'm a sensitive man and I've just contributed my sadness or emotions to it but I've realized that I too have a broken cup. I'm sure you didn't really think that you were going to reach me of all people, but I still can't get over how much you have challenged me.

God really wanted me to be there, in what I thought was for you. It was very hard to hear you outline what you have been through for the past four years. I can't believe the strength you have. It makes anyone find a way to survive, to reach down and make a change, a difference. . . . After hearing you speak, I realized why you have such strength. I too believe God has lifted you up and will continue to provide for you. It's easier to say but harder to come to grips with.

Finally, it is as overwhelming to me as I know that it is for you to see what an impact you have had on the many thousands of people across the world. You have such a gift and you are doing exactly what God wants you to do. The lives that have been changed, the people that now have hope and a way to change . . . that is the most incredible feeling, to know your mom, Brad

Barnes' mom, is the one who has directly had life-changing impact on so many people. I can't tell you how proud I am. My heart is hurting and my cup is broken, but I know I can make the changes. I know I have the strength. Thank you for helping me. Thank you for teaching me with your words. Thank you for being my mom.

Love, Brad

How could my cup not overflow with joy over the impact of a letter like that? I am truly overwhelmed to see the ongoing flow of blessing. So many seeds planted long ago are now blooming. So much pain is being redeemed. So many questions are coming clear that I never understood before. I am grateful beyond words for what I believe God is showing me.

And the essence of what I am learning is just this: it's all him. God is the one who is doing these great works, who is forging link after link in the chain of blessing.

My part, again and again, has been simply to trust, simply to obey, simply to remember to praise and thank him for what he has done.

Much of the time, especially in my times of worry and illness and near-despair, I haven't even managed much trust, obedience, or thankfulness.

But God has used my tiny bit of trust, my scraps of grudging obedience, my half-hearted thanks, and he has multiplied these things like loaves and fishes.

There has always, somehow, been enough. More than enough. Again and again, my cup has overflowed with blessing.

So it really is a "God thing."

I can't believe that I, who tend to appreciate the formal, the carefully crafted, the lovely, have taken to using a slangy phrase like "God thing." It doesn't really sound like me. But I use it because it speaks so much of what is in my heart.

It's *all* a God thing—my life, my health, my ministry, my family.

The same is true of your life, too, whether your ministry involves the kitchen or the speaking platform . . . or the daycare center or the employees' lounge. Whatever your walk in life, and whatever the trouble that may be filling your cup right now, God is still in the process of doing an amazing work in your life. Because he is God, because he's in control, because he's infinitely good and loving, we can trust him to forge link after link in the chain of blessing.

And so I'm not quitting, not by a long shot.

But even when I do retire, whether it's to my little kitchen or to my heavenly Father's mansions, I know God's chain of blessing will go on and on . . . through the pain and suffering that inevitably afflict us on this earth, filling our cups with trouble, and on into the future of overflowing blessings that he has prepared for all those who love him.

It's All You, Lord!

Some Words to Praise
the One Who Can Do It All . . .

Many, O Lord my God,
  are the wonders you have done.
The things you planned for us
  no one can recount to you;
were I to speak and tell of them,
  they would be too many to declare.

Psalm 40:5

As it is written:

"No eye has seen,
  no ear has heard,
no mind has conceived
  what God has prepared for those who love him"—

but God has revealed it to us by his Spirit.

1 Corinthians 2:9,10

Do we need, like some people, letters of recommendation to you or from you? You yourselves are our letter, written on our hearts, known and read by everybody. You show that you are a letter from Christ, the result of our ministry, written not with ink but with the Spirit of the living God, not on tablets of stone but on tablets of human hearts.

Such confidence as this is ours through Christ before God. Not that we are competent in ourselves to claim anything for ourselves, but our competence comes from God. He has made us competent as ministers of a new covenant. . . .

2 Corinthians 3:1-6

Praise be to the God and Father of our Lord Jesus Christ, the Father of compassion and the God of all comfort, who comforts us in all our troubles, so that we can comfort those in any trouble with the comfort we ourselves have received from God. For just as the sufferings of Christ flow over into our lives, so also through Christ our comfort overflows. If we are distressed, it is for your comfort and salvation; if we are comforted, it is for your comfort, which produces in you patient endurance of the same sufferings we suffer. And our hope for you is firm, because we know that just as you share in our sufferings, so also you share in our comfort.

2 Corinthians 1:3-7

I want to know Christ and the power of his resurrection and the fellowship of sharing in his sufferings, becoming like him in his death, and so, somehow, to attain to the resurrection from the dead.

Not that I have already obtained all this, or have already been made perfect, but I press on to take hold of that for which Christ Jesus took hold of me. Brothers, I do not consider myself yet to have taken hold of it. But one thing I do: Forgetting what is behind and straining toward what is ahead, I press on toward the goal to win the prize for which God has called me heavenward in Christ Jesus.

Philippians 3:10-14

It Really Is Too Much, Lord!

It really is too much, Lord.
When my cup overflowed with trouble,
you made my cup deeper and stronger.
You washed it free of trouble
and filled me to overflowing
With your goodness,
and you keep on doing it
every day of my life
even when it's raining.
You are a God of abundant mercy.
You are a God of abundant strength.
You are a God of abundant blessings.
It's too much, Lord.
But thank you!

Epilogue

A Look Beyond the Clouds

$\mathcal{I}$'ve seen it a million times in the years that Bob and I have been frequent flyers. Every time, it has surprised and delighted me. More recently, it has been a source of comfort and encouragement—a mental picture that has kept me going in the rainy seasons of my life.

Here's how it happens.

We drive to the airport in pouring rain, or dreary drizzle, or gray overcast.

We check our luggage as usual, pass through the gauntlet of X-ray checks, wait at our gate while staring out at the now-familiar wet grayness.

We board the plane, stow our carry-ons, glance out through the rain-spattered windows as we fasten our seatbelts.

Then we take off, disappearing within minutes into a blanket of fog.

We glance at our magazines and listen with half an ear to the familiar litany of safety instructions.

And then, just as we're getting settled into the routine, we glance out the window again to see . . . nothing but blue skies and sunshine.

No matter what the weather is like down on the ground, once you get above those clouds, it's always a sunny day!

And it *is* beautiful up there. Seen from above, those very clouds that rained on everyone's parade and dragged down everyone's spirits are soft, billowy, inviting. I find myself wanting to jump down into them and bounce around like a child on a wonderful featherbed.

How can the same clouds look so amazingly different?

It's all a matter of perspective . . . and it's a perspective I desperately need on these days when everything seems dark.

My rainy season, you see, is far from over.

My disease is a chronic one; my health will likely improve and then decline and improve and decline, perhaps for the rest of my life. Even as I write this epilogue, I am going through another time of elevated white counts and renewed bronchitis.

And I have no guarantees that the other kinds of pain in my life are behind me. Neither do you. Neither does any of us.

The Lord said, remember, that in this world we will have trouble. That's a given, an inevitable consequence of living amidst this fallen creation. The rain falls on the just and the unjust, and one good soaking is no guarantee that we won't get wet again.

But that's why it's so important to keep in mind the truth that I learn and relearn whenever I'm given the privilege of flying above the clouds:

No matter how thick the clouds and how hard the rain, you see, the sun is still shining.

At the very same moment that life seems darkest, the sun is dancing beautifully off those puffy, inviting clouds.

Most important, our Lord and Savior Jesus Christ has promised that the sunshine is the place we belong—and the sun is always shining.

"Do not be dismayed," he said. "I have overcome the world."

It's so easy to forget that the sun is shining when the storm clouds loom.

It's so easy to become depressed and discouraged when the rainy season lingers. It's so easy to fall into fear when the low places flood.

But it's so vital to remember, again and again, that the sun has never really left us. Rainy seasons come and go, but even the longest rain is still temporary. It's the sunshine that never ends.

And that is not a pie in the sky, poor-second consolation for people who just can't cope.

That is reality—as strong and shining a reality as the brilliant sunbeams that glint off the wing of our jet and dance on the surfaces of those clouds.

That is a reality I can rest in, bask in, sink into.

God grant us all the grace, at any given rainy moment, to open our eyes to the reality of that life-giving sunshine.